One Paw at a Time

A Tail of Recovery

Jo Sellers

FIRST EDITION
Published in 2025 by
GREEN CAT BOOKS
19 St Christopher's Way
Pride Park
Derby
DE24 8JY

www.greencatbooks.com

Copyright © 2025 Jo Sellers
ISBN: 978-1-913794-93-4

ACKNOWLEDGEMENTS

Being thrown into a disaster can be lonely, but I had the most amazing support, both in person and virtually from a big network of dog lovers, dog professionals, clients and friends.

The quick responses from my local vets that night, and their dedication to keep Reba alive and comfortable, saved her life, and their ongoing patience to all my calls and messages throughout the initial months was invaluable. Their help with the acupuncture meant that Reba was happy in the familiar clinic.

The specialist referral centre was amazing in their skills to stabilise my girl, and the full team from the surgeons, physiotherapists, hydrotherapists, neurologists, kennel teams, and reception, their smiles have made this journey so much easier. Being geographically close to me enabled all these therapies can be continued under one roof and less stressful.

A special mention to Catriona, my McTimoney therapist who still laughs at my very polite message on the night of the accident saying 'only pencil in the appointment next month, we might have to postpone as she's broken her neck' and her weekly trips to treat Reba at my home thereafter.

As for the support to me, it came from my friends and dog network across the UK and the rest of the world. I know that I will upset many as I can't list you all, but I appreciated every single interaction. From Zoe setting up the GoFundMe page to help with the costs, my mentor Julie in Canada and her team, colleagues Rosee, Rachel and so many more, and those that also gifted Reba treats to aid her recovery. I may have physically been alone, but in spirit I had a huge hug daily from all of you.

Accident – Sunday 27th October 2024

It was a normal day. We'd been home from holiday in Cornwall for three days. We went for a walk and she got a bit muddy, so I wiped it off and was going to bathe her the next day (to give her time to dry properly before nighttime).

About 8.30 p.m. on Sunday night, it was dark, and she wanted to go out for a wee. I let her out as normal, she scampered past the patio and onto the grass. I heard a squeal, and I honestly thought it was from a surprised cat or something that she had disturbed in the garden – again, normal! But it went very quiet. I closed the door, and after a minute, I just felt something was wrong but wasn't sure what. I called her, no response, and then I thought maybe she had caught a rodent and was eating it, so she wouldn't respond, even to the treat packet being rattled.

I grabbed my phone, switched on the light, but couldn't see much. It was damp, and I just had my slippers on. So, I went back in to get my back door shoes and ventured further into my garden with the phone torch. About 10 metres in on the grass, I saw her lying next to the small cherry tree on her side. It took a few seconds to realise that she was motionless and that it was serious. I screamed for my neighbours – but then I realised they must have gone away as there were no lights on in their house. Still, I screamed for help but being winter, as all windows were shut, there was no-one around. This was all within four to five mins of letting her out for her wee.

Whilst shouting, I went to press on her chest and felt a strong pulse, but saw that she was gasping/choking and her tongue and mouth was purple. My immediate thought was she was choking and needed unblocking. One way to help dogs is to pick them up by their back legs to help dislodge anything in the airway – this is what I had learnt in canine first aid. However, when I went to pick her up, she was totally floppy, so rather than shake her (and thank goodness I didn't), it clicked in my head that she may have broken her neck or back.

I scooped her up off the wet grass, ran indoors and lay her on my kitchen floor whilst I looked up my vet's number. They are an independent practice and have their own emergency cover, but, out of hours, you have to note down another mobile number and call that. Well, I was so uncoordinated and in shock, it took four dials of their voicemail to jot down that number. Tip – it's now saved at the very top of my contact list on my phone, so no scrolling needed.

They answered very quickly, and although the thought of me driving her and not being able to attend to her at the same time filled me with dread, I agreed to rush her in, after explaining what had happened.

The vet is two villages away, so a 10-15 min drive. It was horrific.

I had laid Reba in the boot, as that is flat, and where she normally goes. It has dividers for safety, as I didn't want her moving off the back seats (this is where my brain was not functioning rationally, as of course she couldn't move at this point if she wanted to).

All the way, I was talking to her – I love you, hang on, Mummy is here, good girl, come on... the last one was directed to both her to hang on to life, and to will the car in front of me to go fast! My prayers were answered - it is mostly a 30mph limit for most of the route, but the car in front (how dare they be there!) were speeding, as was I. Let the police catch me later, I didn't care at that point. My only thought was to get help and some expert hands on my dog. My fear was that she would die alone in the back of my car without me holding her.

I arrived at the vets. They were waiting for me and saw my car fly in and slam to a halt in front of the doors. The nurse came out and I just said 'help me' so she scooped Reba out of the boot and carried her in whilst I closed my car up and held the vet door open for her. They rushed her into the main consulting room, lay her down and instantly put the oxygen on her, so I helped to hold the mask near her face, as Reba was agitated. It was during these first few seconds that I noticed that Reba was breathing better, and her mouth was pink again. I feel my talking to her the whole way helped her to recover that aspect, as they did say it sounded like she was having a seizure after the impact.

The nurse had already paged the on-call vet, and it turned out he lived very close to me as he recognised us!

I was there to reassure Reba, to keep her head still as much as possible, and I went through all the things I had done and seen. They were very complimentary and said my quick actions had saved her life. Had I just gone indoors and waited for Reba to bark at the door to be let in, she would have died in my garden. My gut instinct that night saved me. By now, from letting Reba out, and arriving at the emergency vet, was under 30 mins, it was still before 9 p.m.

They checked Reba's temperature (oh the indignity, but I doubt she felt it!) what seemed like every 10 mins. She was cold, so they put heat pads under her, blankets on top and 'hot hands' (gloves filled with warm water) on her.

I could see that one of her eyes was very white, and they checked it out and it was Horner's Syndrome. This is where the pupil does not react, and for dogs, the third eyelid gets stuck over the eye, a classic sign of spinal injury in the neck.

The vet picked her up to assess her, and she instantly collapsed with no support on her legs, they literally were holding her up. She had nothing on her legs. They put her back on the table, inserted an IV line (no response from Reba to this!), and then took an X-ray. This is where I had to leave the room for protocol. I was allowed back in and immediately went to Reba's head end but almost behind her so I could reassure her and talk to her, and they had space to do their monitoring.

I was shown the X-ray – her neck vertebrae were out of line (stepped) and a piece of bone had broken away underneath the main injury area.

The vet explained to me what he could see, then went to make some phone calls for a neurology referral. It was an agonising wait, as he had

ONE PAW AT A TIME

to send off the X-ray for them to review before they would accept any patients.

It was only at this point that I suddenly started to cry. It hit me just how serious this was, and how life-threatening this injury could be to Reba. I think I was on automatic pilot before, being practical and trying to remember details.

We were waiting for them to call back, but after half an hour, he called again - they had not got the email with the X-ray! So, we redid and had to wait again. The first referral centre called back but they could not see Reba till Tuesday, and it was not a case that we could wait. So, their second choice was contacted, and on seeing the X-ray, they could take Reba at 9 a.m. the next morning.

By now it was about 10.30 p.m. I had called my new neighbours to ask them to check if I had closed the front door, as I had no recollection, and how could I with Reba in my arms? Apparently I had, and they left me a lovely voicemail.

For now, all they could do was to keep Reba still, give her lots of meds for pain relief, and sedation so that she didn't try and move, and to closely monitor her. They would empty her bladder to make her more comfortable – she had already left a trail of poo in my home as I carried her out of the kitchen and out to the car. I had to say goodbye for now, and that was hard. I didn't want to leave her, not only as she is very hyper-attached to me and does find comfort from me, but I was scared that I might not see her again. They promised to call me at any signs of deterioration, so I kissed and stroke her head, whispered to her and promised to see her tomorrow. I refused to say the 'G' word. I couldn't.

Leaving her and driving home was horrific. Tears were streaming down my face, and it felt so alien to be leaving her behind.

I arrived home and immediately went into practical mode to clear up the poo nuggets trail, and then left some messages to a few clients who were expecting me the next day to work, telling them that I couldn't attend to them. They were all understanding. I put out on social media that she had had an accident, and I won't be on socials or responding to messages, and instantly had messages of support and care, although none knew of the details yet.

I felt sick and was shaking and crying. I knew I had to go to bed. It had been agreed that they would have Reba ready for transporting to the referral centre at 8am the next morning, as I would have to drive her there myself. Thankfully it was not far, under 10 miles from my home but I couldn't be so tired that driving would be dangerous. Sleep, no! I was glued to my phone and was very distressed. I was awake most of the night, dreading a call from the vets, but I must have dozed for about two hours maximum, but woke often.

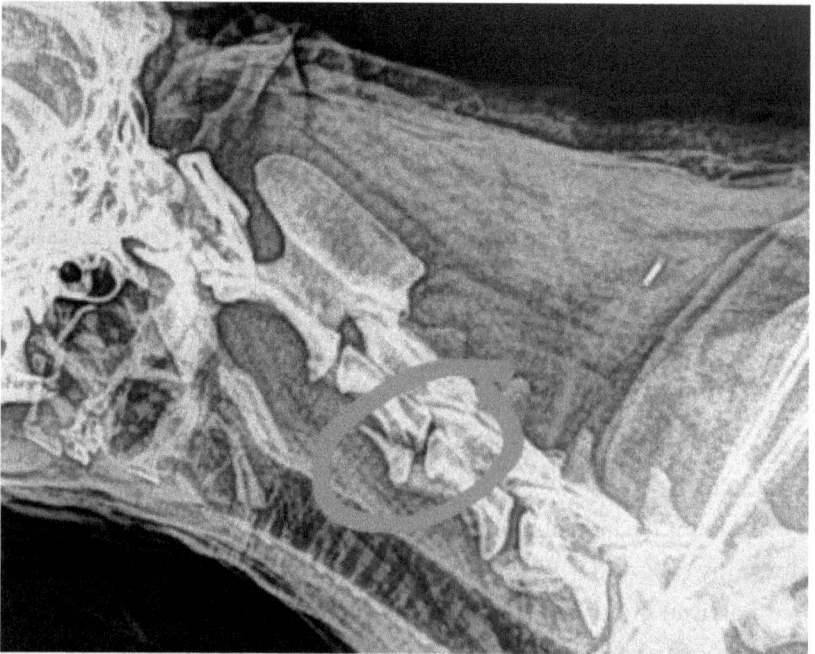

Monday 28th October – admission to the specialist referral centre

By 6 a.m. there was no point trying to sleep, my brain was racing, my tears were flowing, and I was a mess. I had enough sense to shower and wash my hair, as I doubted that this would be thought about later for the next few days.

I wasn't hungry but forced down some toast, as I needed to be on form to do the driving transfer. I arrived just a few mins after the time they needed me – just after 8 a.m. I did notice a missed call later on, but as my hands free/satnav is broken in my car, I couldn't do anything. As I parked up, they were carrying her out of the practice for me, and it was decided to put her on the back seat, so there was more room to keep her laid out, but close enough to know that I am there. That was the second worst journey to date - yes, she was in a more stable condition than last night, she was on lots of painkillers – morphine, Metacam, and sedatives, but it was still a huge responsibility and frightening. I needed to make sure I didn't brake so hard that she moved but wanted to get there fast. A few times I had to reach back so that she could sniff my hand. It was under 30 mins to get there, and finally I found the referral centre. It was daylight, so easier to find as it's a rural location.

I parked up by the reception and went in to announce my arrival. I was told to go and sit down. There was already a couple with a spaniel, and then a lady with poodles arrived. She was struggling to hold one of them, and she was joking that he gets into mischief running into trees. I just couldn't wait there, and didn't want to say anything, and as I was waiting for the receptionist to finish her call to say I would be waiting with Reba in the car, a nurse came out and went with me to see Reba, who was all tucked up and propped up by all the towels in my car. I sat in the back with Reba, until she returned with the neurologist. They checked Reba over, and then carefully slid her onto a spinal board to remove her from the car. They said that my vet had done a good job of packing her in and stabilising her. I followed them as they both carried her into the building and into the consulting room, and they spun the board around so Reba could see me as they chatted about the case.

They looked at the X-rays and said that they hoped to get a CT scan without further sedation. They were worried about anesthetising her for the MRI, as this relaxes the muscles, and it was her neck muscles that were offering some stability to her spine. Once this relaxed, there was a big risk of the vertebrae moving and damaging the spinal cord more, likely fatally. To do the MRI, they needed to wait till they were ready for surgery so they could act really quickly, should that happen.

The consult probably took over 30 minutes, but I really cannot remember much of what they said. I recall that they were impressed I did the right things, quickly, and that my local vet did great - the vet nurse used to work with him, and he was one of the best, so that was good to hear!

They wanted to take her through so that they could continue to monitor her and her pain levels, so I had to once again leave her. It broke my heart, as I knew that I may never see her again, as everything was such high risk. I kissed Reba's head, spoke to her and only told her to be brave and see her later, the 'G' word (goodbye) was too traumatic and final, and I just couldn't go there. Rather than Reba seeing me leave, they carried her on the spinal board out to the medical area, and I went back to the reception area. They had all my towels and Reba's drying robe on the board, as they kept them on her when they slid her onto the board in the car, and I had to wait for them to bring them back – I got the drying robe back but not the old towels!

Whilst waiting, the poodle lady came out with just one (the other one was in for treatment), and her dog immediately made a beeline for me, so I gave it a stroke. When asked, I told her my dog broke her neck running into a tree. Not sure if my words rang a bell to her comments earlier, but thankfully that was when the nurse came out with some of my stuff.

After a little cry in the car, I then had to come home and wait.

I literally could not put my phone down - it was horrific, and I was so distressed.

I called them mid-afternoon, and they told me that she didn't move for the CT scan so that went well, but next was the prep for the MRI and surgery as she will need anaesthesia, but she was doing ok. Her bloodwork had shown a big increase in pancreatitis markers, so this could be a huge risk to her.

I just sat at my dining table, with my phone, like in a zombie state, not moving. The waiting was intolerable, and the worry was off the scale.

All I knew is that they had now gone into surgery and there was nothing I could do.

One thing I had to do was to contact the charity I volunteer for, to take me off the books for a while. I had a prospective volunteer to assess in a few days, so called them to quickly cancel, but they kept me on there for 10 mins, being kind, but it was such a struggle to not break down.

I was getting messages on my original Facebook post saying 'hope she feels better soon', very well-meaning but it felt very disingenuous, and upsetting as I knew it would be anything but, so I posted a picture I had taken of the X-ray from the vets last night, saying she had a freak accident and was now at the specialist referral centre, awaiting surgery (at that point it was not guaranteed they could help her). The engagement on my post was huge, so full of support that reading them made me cry. They still do.

The phrase 'I'm a blubbering wreck' was true, and an understatement. I couldn't think of anything, but anything I did think of set me off crying. I wasn't hungry, struggled with even tea, and really was in a total panic, full of shock.

Early evening, I had a call. She had made it through the surgery, and they had realigned the neck and fused it, and pinned/cemented the broken part back in place. She was still under, and they would bring her around later. They said they would call, but by nearly 10 p.m., I couldn't hang on any longer and phoned them. They had said to call any time, as often as I needed but I also knew they were busy doing their jobs and I was concerned of bothering them.

They said that they were going to include her on their socials, but won't identify me. A friend sent me a link to the story on their social media page, where the surgeon talks about being called to urgently operate on a patient he had never seen before (normally he meets them pre -surgery at least!). They had changed all their schedules to operate on her to save her life. He did name Reba, so my friends knew that this was my girl.

She was in the recovery, doing well and had survived the operation! Phew!

But this was no time to celebrate, it was only the first hurdle of her time there. The next few days were critical, as they needed to see a response from her to ensure that her spinal cord was intact, as well as ensuring there was no infection in the surgical site. They can do their best in the operating room, but there is never a guarantee.

They said they would phone me during the night if they needed me, so once again, I dreaded going to bed but took my phone with me, ensuring it was fully charged.

Once again, I could barely sleep, felt sick and couldn't stop crying. Every normal trick to get to sleep failed, and I was tossing and turning for most of the night. I kept checking my phone, just in case. I think I got a few hours rest but woke up about 5.30 a.m. and once my brain started up, there was no option to stay in bed. I was so scared that Reba wouldn't make it, but there was no emergency call in the night – a positive.

ONE PAW AT A TIME

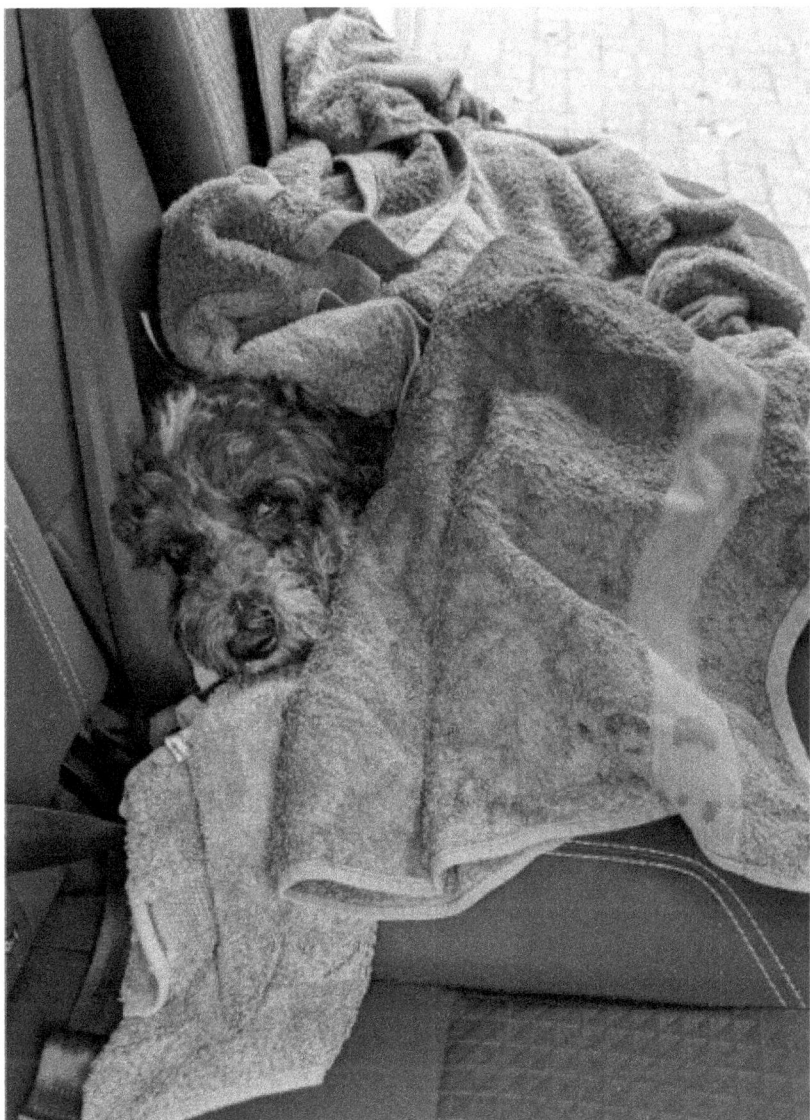

Tuesday 29th October

Sick to the stomach today. I just sat at the table, crying, worrying and really unable to focus on much at all.

I decided to do a quick video to explain what happened. I couldn't deal with contacting everyone individually, and realised that by using my social media, I could keep a lot of my friends and contacts updated, as they are all over the world. It was hard, I was still in my dressing gown, and the tears flowed. And after, I sobbed for hours.

Close friends wanted to help me, and one set up a GoFundMe page as I mentioned that although insured, the cost of the lifesaving surgery was three times the cover limit. It took me ages to be able to read the paragraph they wrote, as I was crying so much. They knew that I didn't have money, and being a sole income, and unable to work now, this would help alleviate some of the financial pressure, therefore allowing me to focus on the practical part of caring for Reba... as long as she came home.

Within minutes, close colleagues and friends had shared the page, and donations started, even from people who had no direct connection to me. It is so humbling.

The neurologist called to say that she had had a comfortable night, her condition remained stable, which was a huge relief, but she needed to show some signs as the first 48 hours were critical if she would regain any neural function.

In the fridge, I had a load of recently defrosted dog food, but on phoning the supplier, they confirmed that it would not last more than a few days in there. As I had been told that Reba will be in hospital for about 10 days, I took some of the food to my neighbour, and took the rest that evening to my vets, so their patients could have a luxury cooked food supper.

The rest of the day was spent just sitting there with my phone. It came with me EVERYWHERE, just waiting for updates. The centre was very good, as they did call me twice a day, mostly once in the afternoon and then early evening for updates, but it was still really nerve-wracking.

I was told that she was lifting her head a bit more, so that was a good sign, but she was still motionless and at risk. There was an update on the referral centre's social page, a story with the surgeon lying next to Reba, who was on her front but literally motionless, stroking her in her kennel (they are really nice ones, not metal bar ones you get normally), and talking about how life is in the balance when you have a broken neck. Reba was awake and moved her head a tiny bit to the side – probably checking to see if he had any treats in his pockets! The neurologist had stabilised her, but he was called into surgery to help as he has experience of putting in metal implants and cement into spinal fractures, and that it is now time for biology to take its course and help the healing.

The team sent me a photo of her in the kennels with the surgeon, for my info. On the one hand, it was lovely to see her but then it really upset me that she was lying there, chin on the ground, unable to move.

The update calls today said that she was eating, and swallowing ok, but her pancreas was inflamed, so possible pancreatitis, or it could be the reaction to the accident, so they will monitor closely. There was also a very small reaction to them pinching and pushing on her front right leg. This is the very first sign that there may be some hope, and her spinal cord is not completely trashed. They are going to give her another day of rest before they start to move her, and get the physio team down to see what she can and can't do. There is a big, experienced team looking after her 24/7, so I have to defer to them.

I was told that I cannot visit her, as they want her to bond with them, so she settles. Given her anxiety issues, if I visit then she is likely to be more distressed when I leave so it's best to keep away. I understand, but this is so painful for me, not seeing her, not knowing and looking at her myself.

I was almost too scared to go to bed, I didn't want to sleep in case they called me, but deep down I knew that she will be watched carefully, fully sedated and pumped with lots of painkillers. Still, it made me feel sick thinking about this, and I had a very fitful few hours of disturbed sleep, waking again really early and unable to stay in bed to try to sleep again.

Wednesday 30th October

I'm a total mess. I miss her dearly. I'm frightened for her, even though she is getting around the clock care and in the best hands. I think I'm still in shock from that night. Finding her, all the stress and upset is taking its toll, and the image of her in the state she was found in is front of my mind. I'm tired, no appetite, but mostly so tearful. I can't concentrate on anything, I don't want to. Every reminder of Reba makes me cry. She's still alive, for now, but her prognosis is so uncertain. She is still critical as there is a risk she won't move or recover, so euthanasia is not off the table, or get an infection that could kill her.

She had her physio assessment today, so they moved her for the first time since her surgery. She's got pins in her neck and fusing of the vertebrae to stabilise her neck, a lot of work done. She apparently has a flicker of reflex on some of her paws, and she wagged her tail! This is one huge sign that there are nerve messages reaching from her brain to her tail, as this move is based on emotions. They are going to try and get this on video for me.

The day is just dragging, as I'm waiting for the next updates from the hospital. I am so upset. I had two surprise deliveries today – a bunch of flowers from one client, turned friend, and a box of dog treats with a beautiful message from the dog of the friend that sent that, which of course made me cry... I just hope she is home soon and able to eat the treats. Reba's situation is still critical. The risk of infection is still high, and of course, if there is no nerve repair that moves her body and legs, then there is no quality of life, and could be put to sleep still. It's so scary.

The update gives me a glimmer of hope, but we are such a long way from saying that she will and can recover. And there is no guarantee that she will be how she was.

It was another dreadful time going to bed, desperate for the phone not to ring (that means it's an emergency in the night) but also unable to sleep for the fear that something may go wrong. I'm too upset to be tired. I hate the quiet. Not that Reba ever made any noise, but it's the fact she is not there. I can't move her bed either, as that seems too fateful and she won't return.

Thursday 31st October

It's Halloween, and it's my nightmare.

Mornings are tough, as I know that they are busy with consults, doing their rounds etc. so I often won't get a call till after lunch, but it's the long wait, willing my phone to ring. I can't think to do anything, concentrate on anything and sit at the dining table motionless for most of the time.

I've started to do updates on my Facebook page - this way I can reach a lot of my friends but without the hassle of lots of messages to each of them. There are others not connected so have to do that, but each time I write something, read something or speak about it, it upsets me too much. I am getting lots of love and support from everyone, many encouraging comments, and the GoFundMe page has been shared extensively by almost everyone I know, and so many are donating, even from those I don't know but just want to help. It's very humbling. Which again, makes me cry!

And embarrassing, I look soooo bad on the reels, hair all over the place, pale, shadows under my eyes, but how I look is the last thing on my mind.

I have a new scar on my head where I was uncoordinated and scratched my forehead getting dressed. I really have no control over my limbs right now.

The update today was better news, her temperature has remained normal so no sign of infection (for now), as the first 48 hours are critical in this regard. On her physio, when they stand her up (very supported by several team members), she is very slowly trying to bear weight on all her paws. She can't support her body weight yet, but there are really good signs, Even on the front left, which has been the least responsive paw till now. It shows she is trying, so there are brain messages trying to get to the rest of her body. It's been a big jump since yesterday, so they are pleasantly surprised and encouraged. They are going to start to reduce her pain and sedation medications, which may increase her anxieties, but they need to try, while keeping the balance to her staying calm and trusting them.

They have anticipated it will be another week, as she needs to be able to squat to toilet, and show signs that she can start to stand, even supported.

Because she had the seizure at the time of the accident, they cannot rule out that she won't have any more, and the pancreas can be affected by the seizures too. But some dogs don't develop seizures. It all depends on how the oxygen supply to the brain was affected at the time, and how it affects them long-term.

It's been another really tough day, I can't process anything, I can't even watch rubbish tv. The neurologist did say she was struggling to send a video of her but will keep trying.

What has helped are my friends leaving voice notes, and of funny anecdotes of what they have been up to. This cheers up momentarily, but I'm still living hour by hour and so stressed.

I did leave a reel with the update, and a huge thank you for the donations. I am insured but the cover limit doesn't even reach a third of what this will be costing me. I can't work right now so very little income too, and will probably have a complete reality meltdown soon.

I have eaten a little bit today, so must be slowly coming out of the shock myself.

Tonight, you can hear all the families trick or treating, but I'm holed up here and don't want to even see anyone.

Friday 1st November

The reception sent me a picture of Reba in her kennel, lying on a few layers of vet bed. This upset me, as in it she is panting, her tongue is quite long and red, and her eyes are wide. I phoned the neurologist to talk about my concern, and she agreed that Reba did not look comfortable. I told her that she is always warm, so they will keep a close eye on her. But she then advised that this picture was immediately after a physio session, so Reba had been made to work a bit hence why she was warm, and right now she was much more settled in the kennel and back to not panting.

After this it was mixed feelings. There is a picture of her, but it distressed me. But it was a recent photo, so that gave me hope.

The days are so long, I'm worrying, and feeling hopeless, and unable to do anything. They are taking better care of her than I could, but it hurts my heart to not be involved.

On the second update call, I did ask about what I might need to prepare for her coming home. One thing that clients often leave to the last minute is consideration of flooring. I have wooden floors, so will need to have less slippery alternatives, so I put out on some local Facebook groups about the interlocking floor mats – suggested by my neighbour. Carpet is too heavy and impractical – especially if she is incontinent. The mats are wipeable, and I can reconfigure them as we need. A friend is sending some that she never used, and someone in my village has loaned me about 25 that were in her garden. They are muddy so need washing, and she will need them back in spring, but this will help me until I can work out what Reba may need longer term.

It is helpful to feel like I'm doing something practical and focusing my mind on Reba's discharge. The rest of the 23 hours in the day is still dragging. I'm getting some appetite back but still not sleeping well and crying lots.

Saturday 2nd November

My main contact, the neurologist had explained that she was away on a 2-day course and the main surgeon and intern will be looking after Reba this weekend. This is the first time I have spoken to the surgeon, and he gave the update that she is making progress as they expect. She is showing some resistance to the right-hand side paws when they press against them, and she has a physio team working with her three times a day, so no rest for her! Her left-side legs are very floppy, but the right-side ones now become rigid – a sign of some nerves working but not enough to bend and flex her muscles and joints.

Sunday 3rd November

Another long day, as the surgeon only gives one update a day, but I did call them mid-afternoon as I was getting worried. They called me back in the evening, and did explain that she is still very ill but stable, and to be realistic in my expectations. I know I need to, but on my socials, I'm being optimistic, however behind the scenes I am very aware that Reba may only have two or three working legs, and might never really be mobile, and still a 'put to sleep' risk. I was sent links to wheels for dogs, but these need two front or two rear legs, however in Reba's case, it's her right side that is showing progress and both left legs that are really weak and less responsive. They are regularly testing her reflexes, and happy that she is making progress.

Monday 4th November

The neurologist told me today that the right side of her body is stronger than the left, so it was likely that she bumped her head more on the left side. She has been lying on her side, and she has a preference on which side, but today she was using her body to shift a bit so that she's angled more on her chest, so lying a bit straighter and lifting her head up. When they take her out on the slings and supports, and manipulate her belly, she is making moves to squat to pee, which is amazing progress. She needs prompting, so not quite able to go totally on her own yet. She is double incontinent and still has no awareness of her bowels. I was told it will take a long time for her to get the sensation, and if she does, then she may never be able to hold it for long, so I will have to be quick!

On a plus side, they normally repeat the blood tests between five and eight days after an operation, so they decided to do this slightly early because of the increased levels and risks shown earlier. They ran them, and thankfully, the pancreas markers were down to almost normal, so there is no risk for her having pancreatitis. This is a huge relief, as it can be a killer, but practically it would have meant a very careful management of food and treats. This is something easily done but given her state, better to not have to deal with an illness on top of her physical and neural issues. Phew.

Tuesday 5th November

At least I don't need to worry about keeping Reba calm during fireworks this week. They tend to go on for about a fortnight, but in her kennels in the centre, and sedated, she won't have a care in the world.

Next door lent me their jet washer so I could clean all the floor tiles. As it's winter, I've brought them all in, propped up against every wall downstairs so they can dry in time for laying ahead of Reba coming home.

I bought some new dog beds in the sale and got some washable pee pads as recommended by friends. Another dog bed has been lent to me from a past client. The other washable pee pads are all ready, one on her upstairs bed and one on the sofa next to me, so I'm getting prepared for her incontinence.

I'm getting mixed messages from the referral centre about when Reba can come home. I told them before that I have a hospital appointment myself on Wednesday, so really would prefer if she was still there so I can go to that, and I have an awards night up near Manchester (I'm a finalist for my business) on Thursday/Friday but this can be cancelled. The surgeon called and said that Reba could be home on Wednesday, but the neurologist said that she preferred Reba to stay longer as she will get more physio and care - the longer the stay the better, so Saturday was her goal. I will just have to wait what the compromise is!

I'm getting really nervous about her return, as I don't quite know what to expect. I can't wait to see her and be with her, but the gravity of the situation is sinking in.

I had a call to confirm that she will be discharged on Thursday lunchtime, so I cancelled the awards night trip, as I will be needed here. I've laid the floor mats down, and got the exercise pen ready in case that is needed to ensure she doesn't move far, but no idea if or when I will need to set that up.

I struggled to sleep again, as I'm just going over in my mind what state she will be in when she comes home. No matter what they tell me in the updates, the reality will be hard.

Wednesday 6th November

Busy day preparing today. Checked that there were plenty of the floor mats down in the areas she will likely be wanting to be near me. This is covering the flooring of the kitchen area to the back door, which is one side of our L shaped main room. The middle bit is normally her 'hang out' area so lots of mats there and a new dog bed – one that I got in the sale this week. I have set up another area by the dining table/ behind my desk and the new vet bedding should arrive any day now.

I had my hospital appointment this afternoon and was dreading it as the consultant has not been particularly nice or helpful, since last treating me two years ago. This time though, he was a totally different person – I was so shocked. Not only has he finally recommended more treatment but gave a prescription too. Sadly, only the hospital can dispense, and their waiting time was hours – it was already nearly 5pm. I took the token and said I will collect the next day – it will only be a quick journey down the dual carriageway to get to the referral centre tomorrow, but tonight I've an electrician coming over to quote for a powerful external garden light. I ran into the supermarket next door to the hospital, as I feel this might be the last time I will get the chance to stock up.

So nervous tonight, as on the one hand I'm super excited to see her, but on the other hand, I'm really worried about what to expect and how I will manage. Although they are telling me her progress, the reality may by a huge shock.

Thursday 7th November

Instead of driving up north to the awards night, I'm pacing at home awaiting the time to collect Reba. I've done as much as I can for now, until she comes home and I can see, then, what else should be put into place. I've worked out the timings to go and collect my prescription from the hospital for my sore back, so I'm hoping this reduces the strain that may be coming, and now I need to hang on till then. This is awful, and part of me wants her to stay in their care for longer.

Well, it's time... wish me luck!

I arrived at the referral centre and quickly got directed to the other new reception as that is where the lead surgeon holds their consultations. It was really quiet, so I was sitting there and out came a large Doberman with its elderly owners and two interns holding the sling under its back end to help it to walk out to the car park. This made me cry, as I suddenly realised that Reba won't be walking. Despite seeing some TV programmes where dogs have had surgery on their necks, and could walk in a few days' time, I really thought that this would be us, but it suddenly dawned on me that life won't be that easy, and that Reba is still paralysed. My heart sank. I suppose I just wanted to be optimistic, but reality bit hard.

Then I heard my name, so walked to the consulting room where the surgeon who operated actually met me for the first time. He said that he was super confident that I could cope because of my background of being a dog trainer, but I wasn't so sure – I've never looked after a sick dog before, and not one so critically ill and needing intensive support.

The neurologist saw us in the main reception, as I had previously told her that Reba was being discharged today so she very kindly had cleared her diary so that she could come into the consult, which was very reassuring as we had been talking lots, and she was the first one to care for Reba when she arrived there.

First of all, they sat me down and started showing me the CT scan and MRI scan results post-surgery. The first MRI showed the spinal cord damage, and they explained what they thought happened – that the sudden bend in her neck stretched the cord and then pinged back, causing the vertebrae to be out of line. There was about an inch of white on what should have been all black along the spinal cord. This is like a contusion, the damaged area, and sickening to see. I didn't get a picture of this, as they moved on to the other scans which were so clear and detailed – better than the human ones! There were lots of pins in her neck, about eight in that one vertebra that broke, and held in by a lovely large lump of cement. This is fusing her neck and keeping the pins steady whilst the bone has a chance to heal.

Now for the main event, they went and got Reba, and I took some sneaky photos of two of the three scans they had left up on the monitors. The door opened... she was being carried in by some of the team and even moved her tail. She looked so happy to see me, and they laid her down on the floor and I went over to see her. The surgeon kept two interns there, one to hold Reba and the other to video it so they have a record of things. I asked to also record as I wanted to not only watch but to play back, as I knew I would forget everything. They started by showing me the physio. It was very clear that Reba could not take any weight on her legs, she was flopping over all the time, and this scared me – they have two people holding her, I will only have myself to hold her AND to do the physio. I needed to manipulate movement on her legs individually and support her into a standing position as part of the initial programme. They are all experienced with these exercises, I've never done this before and I must have looked panicked, but I kept recording so I could see how they were doing them, and where and how to support Reba, as they tried to show me ways of holding her if I was on my own. They explained that right now, she could lie on her side, but she was showing signs of some reflex on her right-hand side paws and offering up some resistance when they push against them. Her left was still not responding, and she had no awareness of toileting, but given support, she was starting to squat to wee.

Anyway, all this movement triggered her bowels, because as he lifted her up to give to me, she pooped all down his legs! It made us all laugh as he was holding Reba, but the intern was going to wipe him down, much to his anguish! They rushed to get me a pee pad (I had none prepared at home, so they had a bag ready with some in) and then placed her on my lap. They wanted a photo, but I told him to keep away from me – he stunk! Reba's poo was quite sloppy and stinky, I have no idea what they had been feeding her on! He said that he'd never been told to keep away after saving a dog's life – he's more of a hugger! He managed to manoeuvre himself so that he could hide the poo down himself, enough for a picture anyway.

I was so scared, they were completing the handover for me, going through all the meds, even giving me extra wipes for her bottom. The neuro mentioned she had some physio cushions that could help support Reba's body whilst I do the exercises, so she went off to get them. I had a good chat to the team, probably inane small talk but he asked me about my dog training and doing the separation anxiety work – they have lots of patients suffering from this.

The physio supports arrived and they demoed with Reba (whilst I videoed), so I had a clearer idea on how to use them solo handed. She really had no awareness of her body, her toes knuckled over and legs and hips slid sideways as she had little muscle tone and no neurological awareness.

I had quite a lot of stuff to get to the car, so they helped me whilst I carried Reba. They lent me the harness (just as standard fleece one) and a sling for her rear end as well as the pads, cushions and meds. She is normally in the boot, and there are guards in place, so we packed in some towels (yes, I had to replace the ones they took when she was admitted!), as I didn't want her rolling around. They loaded up the rest of the stuff and then I was on my own. Yikes. I can't really describe the mix of emotions, from one minute so happy to have her with me, next so worried that she was not out of risk due to infection, or if she never recovered enough mobility then she would be likely put to sleep, and then so daunted about my task ahead – full-time care to a quadriplegic, double incontinent dog.

I also had to pay the balance for her surgery and aftercare before I could leave. OMG, this life saving surgery is not cheap, and I felt really sick handing over my card. I have NO savings left at all, and this won't be the last of the costs, as they want me to start hydrotherapy next week. This will be the best course of treatment to begin with alongside all our homework. I'm prepared to do all I can at this crucial early stage. She needs the healing help now, not next year when I can save up some money for it (after these fees, and the fact I can't work and earn whilst I'm caring for her, being self-employed, it will be more like several years!).

The drive home was slow and steady, talking to Reba the whole journey. I parked on my drive and took a few deep breaths before unloading all the bits, then scooping up Reba, bringing her in and laying her on her new bed in the main room.

I lay down next to her – she was trembling, squeaking and looking really distressed. I did a short video, as I wanted to use this not only as a document of her recovery, for my memories but also as a way to communicate to my bigger network via my social media. Many have been wishing us well, so this is a good option to reach many people without having to do lots of individual messages, which I really don't have the mental capacity to do right now.

It quickly dawned on me that we won't need the x-pen right now, Reba literally cannot move. She's on three types of medication about five times a day so I won't be leaving her alone often. I also need to bring her water and hold the bowl, bring her food, and take her out, but to be honest, how often do we pay attention to when our dogs need a drink, or the toilet? Not so much I guess, and I wish I had. This was freaking me out!

Now I needed to be there for every need, and get to grips with holding a harness and a sling, and straighten her legs, and try and cue her to toilet. I had no idea if she remembered the cues, and less certain if she could action them as her body control was zero.

When I picked her up, she was like jelly, really limp and wobbly. And she pooped all over the floor! Again, stinky, wet and smelly from the food they gave her. I held her against me, and she flopped her head against my shoulder. Tears came to my eyes, as she has never done this before! She is not one for being carried if there is an alternative, so for this to be like a cuddle was so heartwarming, but bittersweet as she can't hold her head up by herself very well.

Using the harness and sling was so cumbersome when the dog has no body strength. She was just swinging, curling around and then crashing down, and I had to find a way to hold her weight (dead weight!), change hand position to hold both with one hand as I tried to at least stop her legs crossing over. Oh my, this was not easy - my back was screaming in pain, and It's still a lot of weight. I have NO idea how I'm going to cope.

When I'm not carrying her (I've been taking her out every hour or two, but no wee yet), then she is lying flat on her side, so I've used a towel as a pillow to support her head. She has a preference to lying on her left side, so her stronger right legs are on the top.

For food, she normally has dry biscuits in the morning with salmon oil, and often vegetables, and in the evening, she has her pouches of fresh, cooked, soft food, which she devoured that night, with me holding the bowl for her as she ate laying down.

In the evening, I moved her to the flat bed in the living room which is right by the sofa, so I can keep a really close eye on her.

Of course, being this time of year and dark, I found my old headtorch, so at least I can see what we are both doing when I take her out at night. I must have carried her to the grass lawn about six times since coming home, each time a struggle but still no toileting happening. She's on pee pads, just in case but no, nothing. Dry. I was told she could squat and wee but it's unlikely she can tell me when she needs to go, so it's a case of going out often. They can stimulate her bladder, but this is not something I can do, nor do they recommend this.

At bedtime, I was unsure what to do. Given that she could not move, I decided to layer my bed with pee pads on top – the washable ones are great as you can get large sizes – and put this right next to where I lay. This way she is close, and I can keep an arm on her to ensure she doesn't move. She had her final meds for the day, some really hardcore stuff, but as soon as we went upstairs, she was panting, whining, wide eyes and was very distressed. This only got worse when I turned the light off. The accident happened in the dark, and despite a ton of sedatives, she was alert and scared of the dark.

We didn't get much sleep, as she was anxious, I was awake for most of it, worrying, and to be honest it was a wretched night. I really doubt if I can cope with this and feel very out of my depth.

I'm not a morning person but we were up early, as lying in bed was not really working.

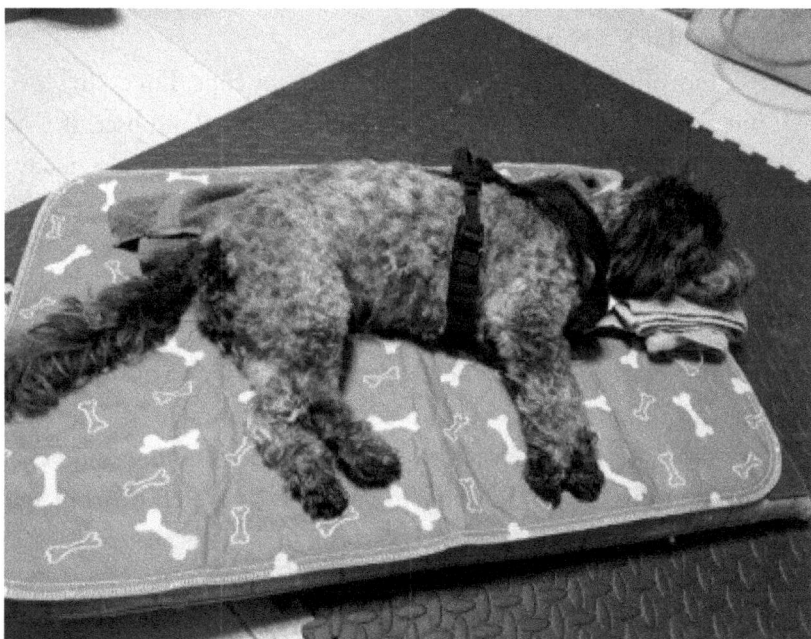

Friday 8th November

Horrific – I feel so bad because I cannot cope. I'm crying lots still, but trying not to as I don't want Reba to sense I'm upset. If I've ever cried before, she gets anxious, and that is the last thing she needs right now.

One positive, she did not wet the bed. On the negative side, she still has not done a wee since I picked her up. I will give it till lunchtime, as they had expressed her bladder before I collected her yesterday, but holding that much wee is not healthy and can cause a bladder infection. She is on enough meds without adding antibiotics into the mix.

Tried her with a small breakfast, but she took one snuffle, about two mouthfuls (the bits with the meds as I covered them in squeezy cheese) and refused the rest. I will speak to the referral centre later with my concerns on both of these issues.

Another obstacle I had not prepared for, was my care. Reba is so vulnerable and scared that if I even leave her side, she freaks out. This makes going to the bathroom, let alone time for a short shower, impossible. I figured that all my attention needs to go on her, and if I'm smelly, then so be it. Who cares? Any visitors will understand, at least for my first few days till I can figure out how I can go about my very limited routine.

She was quite shivery today, so I covered her with some towels. She's never liked blankets or coverings, and therefore I knew she was poorly by tolerating them. All day, when not being taken out for a toilet attempt, she is just sleeping and so still. It's heartbreaking, and I'm desperately worried.

Outside, I've positioned one of my garden chairs to be on the edge of the patio, so that I can sit on it whilst holding Reba. This should help my back, and use my arms supported on my legs to take some of the strain of holding her. Being winter, the metal chair is freezing, and I tried a towel down as it had morning moisture on it. Well, that didn't work, as the wet went though and onto my jeans, so now I have a wet bottom! I have a dry robe coat, and despite being tall, thankfully it still covers my bum when I sit down so that is now at the back door, ready for use each time I take her out.

On that note, I must have taken her out every half hour! Nothing. I am getting worried. This went on all day, but she did eat her dinner. All she did all day was lie in the bed and shiver. She hardly moved, she was resting lots, but it was scary seeing her so still and inactive – she is half-spaniel, and half-clingy bichon that moves when I do, so lying still for that length of time is not normal. I know she is on sedations, but this is really disconcerting as reality is hitting that this is our life now, for the foreseeable at least.

It got to early evening so I called the referral centre, and there was an intern covering for the surgeon this weekend and he suggested I come back in so they can express her bladder. They are about a 20 min drive away, so we went down there and they took her through to help her. As soon as they started, she squatted and boy, she needed to go – their words! We talked about her distress at night, and they offered me up some different meds that sedate her but also will relax her muscles more so she can toilet by herself again.

Off we went home again, still unsure if or when she will toilet next. I tried again that night but partially expected nothing to happen after earlier.

That evening, I laid her on the sofa next to me – under a pee pad of course – so that I could keep her close, and this is more normal for her anyway. Already, you can hardly see her wound. There are about two stitches showing at the top and bottom of her neck, and the cut was about three to four inches long on the underside of her neck. Her hair is already growing back. Incredible. They made a very neat job of the shaving area too, she has a little goatee under her chin and very straight lines down her neck.

I feel like a zombie. I'm incredibly tired, after not only last night but the last 10 days of worry and sleepless nights. I've been in shock and gone through a trauma as much as Reba has, but she's had meds to help her rest. I have no idea what I'm doing, and struggling to focus on anything, even on a TV programme. I can't even think about my business, but I do have some clients ongoing who are aware of my situation and honestly have been fabulous. They are patient as they know I am less reliable, and sometimes a bit late with their plans and updates.

Saturday 9th November

A dry night, but I know I'm on borrowed time!!! She was right next to me on my bed, so I could sense when she was awake, and could reassure her when she was distressed as she is not liking the dark. I think there is some level of PTSD trauma with the dark. I'm too scared to move myself so it was not a good night for me and hardly slept with worry.

Downstairs, I moved her bed closer to me as I sat at the table, but she just whined and squeaked. Her breathing was rapid, licking her lips and her eyes were very wide. It's sad to see, as there is not much I can do to help her. She is petrified. Dogs don't understand injury or rehab, all she can sense is that she cannot move, at all, apart from lifting her head. It upsets me to see her like this, and I have no end date in sight.

I have a client discovery call, so not a long chat but Reba was so distressed, I had to pick her up and put her on my lap, with a pee pad just case, otherwise her crying was getting worse. She will normally lie on my lap when I'm working but this time she was so floppy and it's hard to hold her.

I'm taking her out almost every hour, and hope she will toilet by herself today. My prayers were answered after lunch, and she made to squat to wee, however I have to support her full body weight. I'm saying my cue so hopefully the old association will kick in. The blocker is that the messages from her brain are not getting to her body or her legs so even if she is mentally trying, her body is not listening and so not reacting as she intends. What she has tried today is to move forward when I'm holding her on the grass. Her strongest leg, the front right, is making moves to stride out, and two other legs are twitching which means she has intentional thoughts, and that some messaging is getting through the spinal cord in the neck. She is not interested in any toys or even chews at the moment. A lovely supplier sent a huge box of natural chews for her so I'm sure she will appreciate these soon.

I called the referral centre regarding the meds, as they are not keen to put her back on the trazadone as it causes muscle tension and is stopping her peeing, and this can cause a UTI if she cannot regularly empty her bladder. It's either having her passed out and unable to toilet, or able to toilet better but her being distressed. I'm not sure what the solution is right now.

I'm getting lovely messages of support from friends and colleagues, each one makes me cry. There are also lots of donations coming in, which is really humbling that both those I know and those I don't all want to help me. It's hard for me to look right now, it's a strange position to be in but it's helping me feel less isolated.

I've been messaging a few close friends, but struggling to muster the rest so I expect they understand that this is really hard to focus on communication right now.

A friend came over for a short while to help with the physio exercises, by holding Reba whilst I could manoeuvre her legs. Reba was so excited to see her and was wagging her tail lots. My friend helped me with her in the garden and had the magic touch – Reba actually squatted and weed! She suggested trying her in the buggy, so we worked out how to set it up, put Reba in there and gave her lots of treats, and it seems to work. She seemed happy to lie in it so will try it for real soon outside.

This evening, she was curling up a bit on her side when she was next to me on the sofa, almost having her nose by her rear legs. This is incredible given what she has been through. Her legs are just stuck out, but she is trying to move her body, and that makes me happy. All I want is her to keep progressing, to give us both hope. She was on a pee pad, and had a towel propped under her head, and a cover over her to keep her warm.

And finally, she was snoozing, as she has been restless all day, not happy and whining. It's so distressing for me too, as I just can't help her understand the situation we are in. There is a box of tissues near me in every room, as randomly I will cry, as well as whenever I see any messages or comments, thinking about the mess we are in.

We seem to have a new routine at night. Reba is distressed still, and often poo slips out. She is back on just her fresh cooked food, as we were recommended to only feed her soft food for now as her throat heals, and thankfully this causes easy to clean hard nuggets! When she needs a wee, I also get no indication, she just raises a leg if she is lying down so I have her waterless foam shampoo and towels, and lots of spare pee pads by the bed as well as downstairs. It's hard work cleaning up and shampooing her legs in the early hours of the morning.

Sunday 10th November

I'm not feeling any better about caring for Reba!

It's so hard holding her for toileting, knowing when she needs to go – so we are out about six times for every wee, holding her for physio and literally just caring for her. It's the most challenging thing ever, and such an emotional rollercoaster.

For the physio, I need to hold her up, so she is standing and straightening her legs, and her paws are in contact with the ground. I then need to take one leg at a time and do 'cycling' motion, so stretching her leg forward, sliding it back along the floor, bending it and then stretching it forward again. She cannot take any weight and as soon as I take a hand away to sort a leg out, she flops over to one side. The physio cushions are not much help – one is too low and one is just too high, so her paws don't reach the floor! A friend suggested finding some kind of storage box that is the right height, so after an extensive search, I've found a washbag that is the right height and spread, and I can fill that with towels to take her weight more.

I need to do these exercises a few times a day, but it's super hard with only one person. A few friends have offered to help, but as there is a nasty flu/cold bug going around, many are cancelling as they appreciate that getting ill is the last thing I need right now.

I have lots of enrichment toys and scentwork kit, however it's amazing how much needs either standing up, or some kind of dexterity. She has neither and we are very limited. She is depressed, unsurprisingly, and there is not much I can do for her just yet. I know in my heart that once she can take some weight and even move more (so less reliant on me holding her – which I can't do for long as I get shooting pains in my back), then she will feel chirpier and do some enrichment and start being happier. She can only lie on her side for now.

My next-door neighbours came round – I invited them over as they have been so upset with all the news, and their daughter, who adores Reba, has been particularly distressed. In the end, it was just the mum and so she came in to see Reba, who was wagging her tail in excitement. I got her to video Reba and also when I picked her up to get her 'standing' but fully supported so that the daughter could see that Reba was recovering. Afterwards, they sent a message to say that they were all overjoyed to see her, and the fact she is well – all things considered.

On the plus side, she managed two wees today, so relief for me, and for her. She is super clingy, though, and squeaks and whines even when I leave a voice note or take a phone call.

At bedtime, she is still quite distressed. She is on the bed next to me, and I am having to keep my arm over her to reassure her. The new sedative meds are supposed to help her but also help her toilet better, but they don't seem to have much effect on her ability to sleep at night. It's hard to know what to do, as I need some sleep too. It's exhausting physically and mentally looking after her and carrying her around. I was, however, impressed but also very annoyed as she managed to curl around, raise a leg and do some 'lady grooming' – right by my head!! Grrr but secretly proud that she is able to do this!

Monday 11th November

She's still not so keen to eat breakfast, but she will eat by evening – maybe she may lose a bit of weight to make it easier for me! Because she has no core strength, she is a dead weight to lift.

On the Diazepam, she is more awake, more fidgety, and also if I try to lie her on the other side, she is shuffling back to her preferred side, but not all her legs follow her, so I have to pull them underneath her body to ensure they are all on the same side. It's making her more distressed unless she is on my lap, making even a bathroom trip problematic for me.

I decided to try out the buggy today. It's cold but sunny and we can both do with some fresh air and a walk. It's quite heavy to lift in and out of the car, but if I can operate it and she stays put, then fabulous. There is a tarmacked path around a lake a short drive away, with a café truck by the car park.

Managed to park, open up the buggy and put Reba in. I covered her in a bath towel to keep her warm, and went for a potter. My steering is shocking! I did attempt to get her nose near some bushes so that she could have a sniff, but she was not interested.

One thing I found hard is that a few people on the route saw us and stopped to ask if she was elderly. When I briefly said she was recovering from a neck injury, they wanted to talk but I couldn't. I had to keep it really brief as I could sense I was breaking down. As soon as they were out of sight, the tears were rolling down my face. I just can't talk about what happened, however I keep being asked.

It was a nice walk, not far but the plan was to sit and have a coffee, however Reba got whiney in the buggy, so I ordered a coffee and sat in the car with it, as madam was happier there than outside.

Not bad for a first attempt, and so glad that this was lent to us as otherwise we have no way of getting outside and have no idea if or when Reba can walk again.

The fresh air did us both good and was nice to get out at last.

Back home, she had her head on my lap on the sofa. I put a towel under to support her, to keep her neck more straight in line with her body, and another over her to keep her warm, and she slept a bit. This meant I couldn't move, but was a small sacrifice worth making.

One of my contacts talked about electro-acupuncture, so asked the referral centre about this. Also contacted my local vets – one of them is a trained acupuncturist, so this is super handy as they have all her medical notes and scans from the hospital. It's easier to keep things all centralised as otherwise I have the hassle of trying to pass notes from one place to another.

Looking around at harnesses with a handle that is far enough down the back to hold her stable, but one-handed. What a nightmare this is, as all of them are so short in the body, it won't work. Ordered one that might work, so fingers crossed. Using the normal harness and sling is hard, because she is trying to turn around and it's twisting in my hand, and that is painful. One progress, though, is she did a wee and a poo just one after another, and in response (I hope) to her toileting cue. It's been a few days since she did a poo so that is good. She is really wobbly, but she seems to be able to take more weight on her front legs (still with knuckled over paws) but her hips swing from side to side, no stability there yet.

Reba is still distressed at night, and wakes every hour or so, and that is after she eventually sleeps. I don't think the change in meds is a positive one so will speak to my vets on this matter too. I'm also grateful for double pee pads on my bed! And plenty of spares to hand as she has no awareness of poos, and for the wees, she can't get up so just raises her leg, making a mess on her. I now have a bottle of enzymatic cleaner both upstairs next to my bed and downstairs – covering all incontinence accidents!

ONE PAW AT A TIME

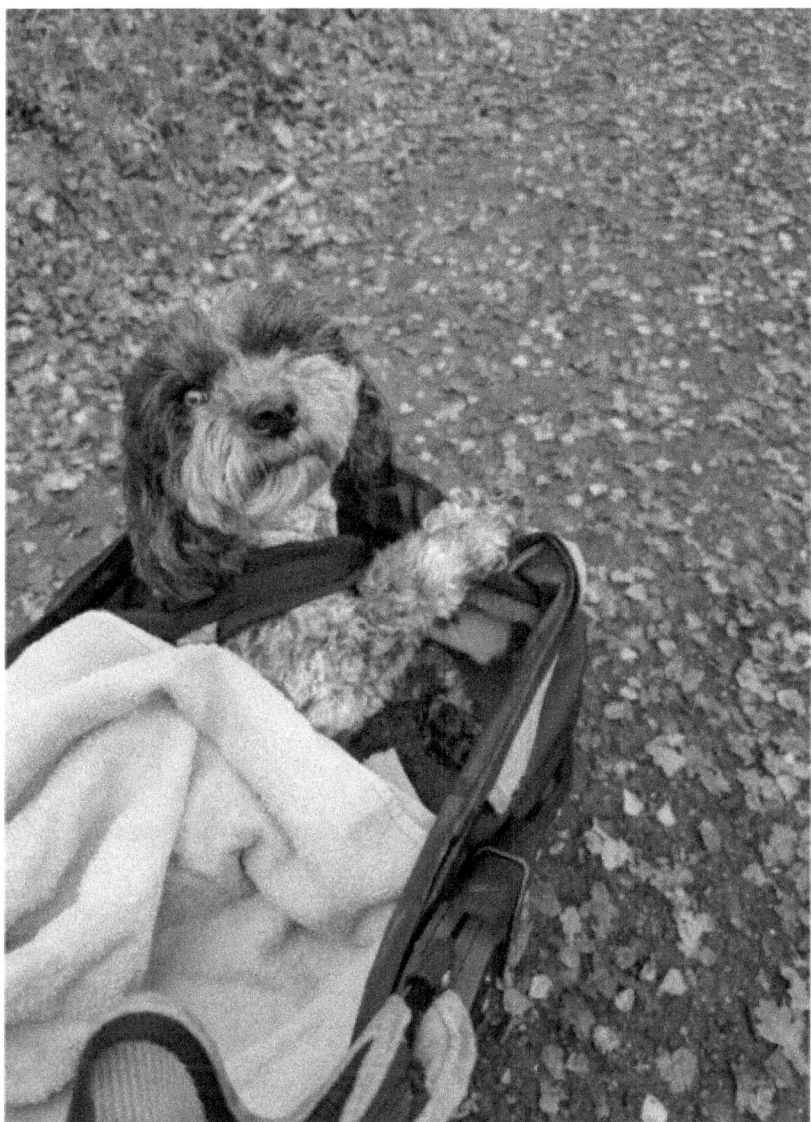

Tuesday 12th November

It's now dangerous carrying her downstairs in the morning, as there are flying poos everywhere! I need to be really careful where I stand, and then once she is on the bed downstairs, I can retrace my steps with poo bag in hand. This is our new daily routine!

My car was booked in for MOT and service, and I phoned the garage to explain and that I will have to cancel or just do the MOT and use the buggy to loiter in the village whilst they work on it. They were so lovely and offered to pick up and collect – a service they don't normally offer as they don't have the staff members to do this. Getting the car sorted is then one less thing to reorganise in my life.

In the garden, she is starting to get some more core strength as she is holding her body better when I pick her up. She is holding her paws in place a bit better now, a few seconds before they wobble and she slides around, and I'm taking every little bit of progress as a positive, no matter how small.

She still flops her head against my chest when I pick her up and I'm making the most of these cuddles.

One thing not improving is her vocalisations, she still whines a lot because she is scared and vulnerable. I'm trying to be strong near her as she has never liked me being upset, but it can be hard to stop the tears during any messages or phone calls. I suppose my way of coping is to appear strong to others, it makes me focus as throwing myself around in floods of tears is no help to Reba. I did so much crying in the first two weeks, and need to concentrate on the practicalities as much as I can now.

Wednesday 13th November

Big day today, as she is back seeing the surgeon to have her sutures removed. I went to the main reception, but they directed me to the new posh one, where the head surgeon sees his clients. The car park is between both, so I was able to get Reba from the car on the way to the second reception. She was just sat on my lap, and there was no-one else there so really quiet! Eventually got called in and was greeting by big smiles by the team as they saw Reba.

They were surprised how hidden the stitches were, what with all the hair growing back already but Reba was really good. I held her on my lap with her chin up, so the intern could remove the stitches, and the surgeon was chatting and watching too. The healing is so impressive, as you would never know that just 14 days earlier, she had a huge slice opened up in her neck. All she has is a lump (like an Adam's apple) on the underside of her throat as the only sign that something has happened, but this is not visible, you have to feel it.

They did a quick assessment, checking the feeling and strength in her legs, and they are optimistic that she is likely to make a reasonable recovery in all her legs, even the current dodgy ones. This makes me so happy. They also said we can start other therapies now too, as long as they keep away from her neck. This will include starting hydrotherapy, and she's allowed to have McTimoney massages.

I want to throw everything I can at her for the first three months at least, so that she has the best chance of recovery, especially for the neural pathways to get the right messages sooner than later. It will be expensive and exhausting but very exciting that we can really get into her rehab. We are doing our physio homework, so fingers crossed that all this effort on her rehab pays off.

Thursday 14th November

My mum came over to visit us, bringing a big bag of food and cake to keep me going. She's never really been a dog person but does love Reba and so she was very concerned about both of us. This visit gave me a little lift, as it can be quite lonely each day coping on my own, even if I do have lots of non-local and international friends cheering me on virtually.

There have been a few toileting accidents today, and we are into the routine of finding our way through the physio exercises as best we can, often combined when I'm holding her over the grass waiting for her to toilet; multi-tasking where I can.

Friday 15th November

I had to do some work calls and Zoom consultations today, and Reba spent all that time flopped over my lap, as it's the only place where she doesn't whine when I try to do some work.

She had her McTimoney treatment today. It's a holistic chiropractic/massage technique so she had a check that her spine was aligned. It wasn't, so she had a few gentle adjustments done on the rear half of her back, but she had a lovely massage to aid the muscles and promote both blood flow and nerve stimulation. We will be getting these treatments weekly as I need all the help I can get.

Spent the afternoon filling in the forms for the insurance claim but need the medical history for her to complete it. They have provisionally said there was no issues with this and were quite surprised at the bills as they were over my cover limit. Life-saving complex surgery is not cheap, and it means that I can't claim for any of the treatments as I have maxed out my cover limit.

Saturday 16th November

A good friend (and dog trainer) came back today for moral support as well as helping with the physio. She is a safe and trusted pair of hands and this really supported me. This is her second visit and offered to come again when she could to help me. We managed to sort out the cushion that supports Reba's body weight whilst I manipulate her legs, and if I use my legs as a guard, then she stays fairly straight for the exercises. A small success!

Sunday 17th November

Another friend drove over with homemade soup and curry and bread/veg bits – so kind and very helpful, as that will be six meals. I've really only been snacking a bit so some better food will keep me healthy. The last thing I want to do is to stand over a stove cooking. Her partner had a horrible accident including neurological damage, so she knows what I am going through, and that we don't even think about looking after ourselves, as all our attention is elsewhere. She appreciated the food parcels at that time, so she wanted to show her support by doing this for me. She also brought a dog plug-in calming diffuser to help Reba settle.

She helped hold Reba whilst I did some physio, as having extra hands there really means I can concentrate on movement and placement better, knowing Reba is supported and stable (as much as her floppy legs allow). It was good to chat too, although I was on the brink of tears all the time, just discussing our situation and what happened. I really appreciated the company, as it also was a bit of a distraction too from what are very intense days.

Later that evening, my old neighbour's family came over and dropped off some lovely gifts – a soft blanket for Reba that I now am putting over her to keep her warm in bed, some chocolates and some beautiful flowers. They didn't stop for long as she was full of cold and didn't want me to catch anything.

Monday 18th November

Had a video call with a new client today, which was hard to concentrate on due to my lack of sleep at nights, leaving me so tired during the day. Reba was whining so I ended up having her laying on my lap with a pee pad between us. Thank goodness they couldn't see that bit!

It was a horrible rainy day, but we have some exciting appointments this afternoon. First off is the hydrotherapy session. This centre is part of the referral centre, so that keeps all the records in one place and it's easy to get to from where we live too. The surgeon had mentioned treadmill, but they had her down as a full swim, which will give her more buoyancy and they can then see if and how she moves her legs.

They carried her in, and I heard some whining but then it stopped. Apparently, that is when the hot dogs appeared! They held her for four laps of the pool, and then they have an area to do some physio by helping her to stand. They were beyond surprised as she continuously moved all four legs, even the weak one. This is an amazing start, and it shows that there are some nerve messages working their way into her body from her brain.

I gave them her drying robe as she went in, as they give the dogs a quick shower and very quick blow dry before putting the robe on, but as they lifted her out and placed her on my lap, my jeans became very soaked through. I must try bringing a towel for my lap for the next session to keep me drier!

We had an appointment straight after with our vets so a quick dash to get there in time. They pulled up the imaging they had been sent and were pleased with her progress and the reconstruction she had in her neck. The vet said that it was too soon for acupuncture but instructed me to see how the hydro sessions went first before trying this new therapy. Hydrotherapy is really effective so we will take each week as it comes, but good to know what options we have to boost her healing.

Whilst there, we saw the nurse that was on the night shift when Reba had the accident. She was very happy to see that Reba was on the mend compared to when she last saw her. Apparently, she was lying by her kennel that night to calm her and reassure her during the night whilst monitoring her. It made me cry as to her level of care, and going beyond what you expect.

ONE PAW AT A TIME

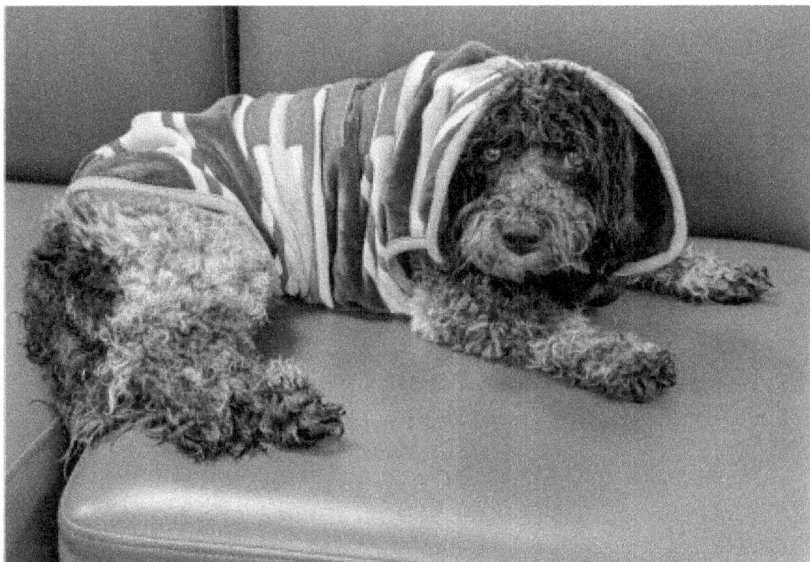

Tuesday 19th November

Bit of a blur day, as we were just resting after her hydro last night, and doing our physio exercises during the day, between taking her out to try and get her to wee in the garden.

As I hold her upright in the garden for a wee, she is now trying to take some steps. Very impressive but making life much harder for me, with the harness and slings getting twisted, and her dead weight straining my arms and back. She is also getting her legs twisted around too, and her front is almost at right angles to her rear, so it's so hard.

I gave her a chew in her bed, and she brought her stronger right paw forward to stabilise it, so that is another progress sign.

Wednesday 20th November

Woke up to poo in her bed, and a trail down the stairs as I took her to the kitchen. She didn't wee when I took her out, and this stresses me more, as it's more difficult to clear up.

I had a new client video call for work and Reba was whining and being so annoying, and when I looked behind me, she was still lying on her side, her leg raised and a huge flood appearing. I had to pause the call so that I could quickly clean up the bed, thank goodness for double pee pads down. Quick towel dry and then shampooed her legs once my call was over. So embarrassing but at least they were understanding.

A friend visited, her dog met Reba at puppy play when they were three months old and have been pals since, but she left him at home this time. Reba was so excited to see her, she did a poo so I quickly bagged it, and as I went out to the back door to place it in the bins, I came back in to find my friend holding Reba half in her arms and Reba wriggling about! She said Reba had pushed herself up to try and follow me, so she just grabbed her. She was super surprised (as was I!) and just how robust she was to what she was expecting.

She gave me a lovely big, snug blanket (waterproof on one side) and some chocolates, which was very thoughtful.

Took Reba out for a walk in the buggy later on and the lovely snug blanket was wrapped around her. She was very happy. I was out of breath and colder! We strolled around the pond, as it has a tarmac path, and saw the ducks on the water. I treated myself to a coffee but had to have it in the car as it was so cold, and Reba was starting to whimper in the buggy.

I had already booked for an oven clean, so the guy turned up but was really kind about Reba, as he had experience of a neuro-injury dog (from IVDD, not an accident). Reba snoozed on my lap and was quite happy.

She was whining indoors, took her out but nothing. Carried her into the kitchen and she was leaving a trail of poo – this is the first time she had any awareness of needing the toilet, so secretly really jumping for joy that she gave some indication, even if our timing was out.

Received her medical records from the vet to send to the insurer (that was another issue as the file was too big, so in the end they contacted my vet directly). It showed that on that night of the accident, she was very distressed – partly from the situation but also the fact that I had to leave her there. They had to give her lots of regular top up medications for sedation and pain, as she was crying, yelping and trying to move. It really upset me reading that, so spent quite a while crying that night.

Thursday 21st November
Reba had her McTimoney massage today. She is not getting any alignment on her neck but the massage on her body and legs is really beneficial, as well as levelling up any lower spine/hip joints. She is quite wonky but as her core strength returns, this should get better. The practitioner has a 'wobbly cat' with neuro issues so understands what we are going through and the limitations of Reba. This session, she noticed that Reba was better, had more resistance to pressure on her paw pads, and also that her 'good' legs were less rigid and more flexible.

It seems that her limbs are going from totally floppy, and showing nothing, to then almost locking and really rigid, to then starting to flex and stretch. Her right front is certainly more the latter, the two other legs are at the rigid stage, and her left hind is still at the floppy stage, so much further behind.

Reba even threw herself off the vet bedding and onto her bed that was next to it. She then was wriggling around on the floor as the massage started but she soon calmed down. I'm impressed by her movement and the determination of her wanting to move and trying, even if she is not successful.

Today was more progress on her incontinence, she indicated twice for poos and once for wees. Not sure if this will last but will take any steps in the right direction.

Speaking to the vets, I was told to start reducing her pain meds, the gabapentin. Reba was so whiney and uncomfortable so this is not a good sign, but we will try and find a good level for her.

Reba is not happy when I speak so every time I do a call, or even leave a voice note, she is whining all the time - until I stop, then she does. Sneaky girl. I can't get angry as she is very scared and vulnerable and needs me.

Tonight, whilst lying next to me on the sofa, she did shuffle across to lie on my lap. Her left hind leg was left behind, but she only does this when she is needing me more or scared. I'm taking all the cuddles I can right now.

When I pick her up, her head flops over onto my shoulder but as she is starting to get a bit more strength, her movements are a bit more volatile and as she is lifting her head a bit more, I didn't realise but ended up with her crashing my face, right by my eye. Bruising is appearing so now I look really bashed up! My forearms are also very bruised too from all the picking her up.

Friday 22nd November

Another disturbed night, but she is still on my bed. I've not had a full night's sleep since the accident and it's affecting me, however I know that once she starts to feel better within herself, we can work on slowly reducing the dimmer switch at night and get her better in the dark. It's just very unclear when this will start...!

Another trainer friend came over today, with some treats for Reba and the extra pair of hands needed to help me with all her physio exercises. We had the excited poo nuggets on her arrival, but she got very fidgety and that has always been her indication for needing the toilet - it's not often we get warning but it's a sure sign the messages are travelling along her spinal cord.

Needed to let a friend's dog out for a lunchtime garden break, so put Reba in the boot of my car as she is much more settled there, even with me out of the car, than being home alone right now. On the way home, we went to the park for a walk with her buggy around the pond for some fresh air. She was a bit whiney but interested in the surroundings. Even odour and different views are enriching for her, and this is all good brain stimulation.

I did a reel of holding Reba on all her legs, and managed to only support her gently as her strength is improving, including her core so that she can hold her body better. She even balanced for a second or two on her own. Can't help but smile, she is turning the corner in trying to heal.

Saturday 23rd November

Stormy day so we are hunkered down inside. Horrible taking her out as I have to be there with her so we both get drenched, well me more so as she is beneath me when I lean over so she is protected from the rain by my body.

Later, on the sofa, the doorbell went, and she tried to get up! She pushed her front legs, so she was lifting her chest off the surface, about halfway up to a sit. Huge effort! She can't hold herself in that position yet, and that little bit of exercise totally tired her out, but I'm so pleased that she could even do this.

Sunday 24th November

Woke up in the night as Reba had moved on the bed. She started out with her head up near the pillow, and her new blanket over her body, tucked up and cosy. In the night, she had managed to get the blanket off herself, turn around and fall asleep with her head pointing to my feet. It is very worrying as I don't want her to shift around to the edge of the bed, or to fall off it as she cannot land or cushion herself, and her neck is still broken despite being pinned. The bone needs to grow together again.

She is showing more awareness of needing to wee, but we get no warnings for poo! Thankfully, due to her lovely healthy, fresh diet, they are super easy to clean as they are solid. Not sure how I would cope if they were soft.

The harness saga may well be over! I've bought (and returned) about four styles of harness so far, including ones that are allegedly suitable for medically challenged dogs. Some had the one handle further down the back of the body, but many had no adjustments for the neck, so they rode up and rubbed her throat, the surgery site. Others, to get the length, were too big, and again rode up her body when she was lying in bed. A colleague sent about six to try but none worked, they were all too short in the body, so when using the handle, Reba was front heavy/rear unsupported and tipped over. I can't use the two-handled one as I need a hand free to keep placing her paws when I do take her out. Finally, one of them had quite a good amount of fabric underneath and the larger size fits her the best. Even on the tightest around her body, it is still a little loose, and the belly strap is still over her ribs but is the longest bodied harness I have found on the market, and believe me, I have tried so many and looked everywhere! This one, the Ruffwear Flagline, supports around the body and stays away from her neck/front of chest so there is no pressure on her pins and cement.

She is now reliably squatting for wees, and she loves to put her (better) right hind leg on my foot as she does so! She is not putting much weight on the diagonal, the front left, so she still needs me to hold her up. Once she can use the left legs more, she will balance better when in this position and won't need my support so much. She is not hunching over yet for the poos, they just fly out! And often I get a trail of them behind me as I carry her out of the home, over the patio and onto the grass. I'm just glad she can go.

Her notification is to whine a bit when she needs to go out, mostly with only a few seconds warning before it happens, but as I taught her as a puppy, I say a special cue word to signal to squat. Well, I've been saying it as she has been and today, I said it in advance, and she duly responded - wow! This time too there was no warning, but she offered the behaviour on the cue. This means that her brain is functioning well again too, so less chance of brain damage after banging her head so hard in the accident (which was enough to smash her neck).

These may be really trivial, and even insignificant things for most owners, but when you have been in a position as we have, this is HUGE! Every tiny detail becomes a win. The one thing that worries me most, more than the mobility challenges, is the incontinence. It's so tough living with a dog that is, and I'm sure we will have problems again as she enters the senior phase of her life, but if we can have a few years of not worrying about it, and not cleaning up after her all day (and night), I will be super happy.

Monday 25th November

I'm really struggling today. The tiredness, the stress and the shock is taking its toll on me.

As soon as we got up and downstairs, she was whining. I ended up taking her out FOUR times in quick succession and each time, nothing. Soon after settling her back indoors, she would whine again. And this is all before breakfast.

I managed to eat, then it was another three attempts. No toileting. It's distressing and it hurts me physically too. My back is so sore, from lifting her, from carrying her, and even the supporting her (standing or sitting on the cold patio chair).

I really feel like losing it. I'm so angry, frustrated and crying. She is not even always holding her body, so she is bending and swinging around when I do hold her up. I can't get angry with her, it is not her fault - well, she should have looked where she was going that night - but we are in this situation and I just have to do my best to help her, no matter how hard it is. Focusing on the practicalities is my way of coping, of focusing myself and keeping my emotions in check so that Reba is not getting distressed.

The whole thing is draining and exhausting, and I'm scared to even think about my finances. I've literally no income, no clients, no chance of working and all my savings have gone on the operation. We have huge therapy bills to come too, as she needs weekly sessions on all the types of therapies, and that is before we add acupuncture later on if she also needs that.

It's been exactly four weeks since her operation, and she is a fighter, but I know it's so hard on her as she must be scared, uncomfortable and confused as to why she cannot move where she wants to go.

The toileting is the hardest, there is no routine to her needing to go, no consistency or schedule, and it's really hacking me off.

Thought I would try and do a bedtime without trazadone. She was ok, a little anxious before we went up but settled her down. She was fine lying next to me as I read, but she quickly got whiney when I switched the light off. She just couldn't settle so I gave her a trazadone pill, finding a bedtime biscuit to hide it in – she spat it out twice but finally ate it. She was just moving around, a few whimpers, and this was the case for most of the night. Woke up around 2.30 a.m., as she was turning around lots, must have done three circuits by morning! But at 5 a.m.-ish, she woke me again, as she had moved to her head being by mine, pushed up on her front legs, and I swear she had also raised her back end a bit too. The outcome – poo! Found out as I reached out to her and put my hand on a little nugget! Thankfully they are quite dry, but I had to get up and collect up the treasures – all were on the pee mat, not my duvet. Tried to settle her again but she woke me a further three or four times.

Tuesday 26th November

I'm sooooo tired today.

Three attempts to get her to wee after breakfast, but still made it out of the house in time for her hydro. We got stuck behind a learner bus, which was super slow, and Reba started crying in the car, but I couldn't stop! Arrived at hydro to some poo in the boot! Once she had gone inside, went to clean the car but the little nuggets had slipped down the gap at the side - she must have kicked them as I lifted her out of the car! Yikes! Reached into the gap to retrieve them, and thankfully again, they are quite hard so easy to hold!

The hydro team were impressed again with her effort. She did some more laps of the pool, and when she stood on their pod, they saw she had improved. She is banana-ing, as she refuses to lay on her right-hand side, so I need to do more of tempting her to look left and straighten her up a bit more.

She was wrapped up and snoozy in the car so took the opportunity to go to the local mini supermarket to grab a few essentials.

Back home, I let her sleep, then gave her a drink. Turned her over – she really protested! Eventually she settled, but as soon as I turned my back, she shifted to lie on her front. Reset her, went to sit down at my desk, and heard a thud – she managed to leap out of her bed and just caught her trying to take a few steps! She landed on her belly and face but about 3ft away from the bed.

I love her fighting spirit and her will to try, but this now starts a whole new set of problems. I was worried she would move off my bed last night, now she will have to go back to hers on the floor (will set some vet bedding around it) but her trying to move before she is able will mean I will have to be extra vigilant, and quick!

Wednesday 27th November

4 a.m. poo to clear up! Was worried about her moving off the bed, but when I tried her in her own, she was whining and panting so she went onto mine again. It was about that time she stirred, waking me up, and managed to resettle her without her moving around. Very tired, but we got up about 8.30 a.m.

Drove to walk on the boardwalk at Thursley – freezing wind but good to get out. Need to step up the physio again – we do lots of standing when I'm taking her outside each time but want to do more.

Had a surprise voice note left for me, a lovely friend who runs a holiday cottage called to offer me a stay there, complimentary, when I feel that Reba is in a position to. This literally brought me to tears. It's up north, in a beautiful coastal village and only a short walk from the car to the cottage (will have to plan luggage and dog!), and a short stroll to the beach. This is so generous. I called her later in the day when I felt I could without crying, only to be told that I've been making her cry for weeks, and she wanted to help me and give me some light and something to look forward to during these dark times.

We just did lots of physio and rest today after the walk, and she was quite good with her toileting notifications.

One thing that she is being a total pain about is lying on her right-hand side, she feels more vulnerable that way as this means her weaker left side is on top, and so she cannot get up. However, what she can do is with her legs straight out in front of her, she will throw her body back and forth till she is more upright, then fling her body around to lie down on her preferred side, however often still carrying momentum and generally falling out of the bed.

The plus side is that all four of her paws now twitch in her sleep, so there is some reaction to her dreaming of running.

She struggled in the first part of the night, waking me before 1 a.m., but no poo accidents, and then she settled until 8 a.m.!

Thursday 28th November

Quite a nice lie in for a change, but she woke me out of a dream with a start, with her shuffling as now she tries to move more - I'm scared she will fall off the bed. She just moved to lay her head on me, but when I got up, I could see she tried to follow me and was creeping to the end of the bed, so quickly grabbed her up and placed her in her own bed (yes, the one she has not been in for a month!) whilst I was in the bathroom, so at least I could relax knowing she is safe. This may be our new routine. There was no nugget trail down the stairs for once, she had her breakfast and even let me finish mine before I took her out for a wee. Did a few physio standing exercises with her indoors and as I was laying her down, she whined so managed to get her out and onto the grass for a poo – first time we've made it in time!!! It's freezing outside, literally!

She did a bit of relaxing on her bed and the winter sun was streaming in and on her, so I think she enjoyed the sunbathing opportunity.

Nana Cake (aka my mum) visiting again today, so heating on, and Reba is resting whilst I'm at the laptop doing a bit of work before she arrives. We were sat on the little sofa, Reba on her bed by our feet and Mum had brought round some sandwiches for lunch. She certainly witnessed the improvement in Reba as the little monkey tried to climb up to get to the food! Mum commented about how last week she was just lying there, but today she was determined to get up, move around more in her bed and generally be more active.

This must be frustrating Reba even more, with her wanting to move but can't. Most enrichment involves the dog standing, so think lick mats, snuffle mats, feeders, even scent detection. There is not much for lying down apart from eating, sleeping, and chewing up all the soft toys she is getting.

It is a sub-zero evening outside, so I've lit the fire, and she is snuggling next to me on the sofa. She even pushed herself by her back legs to climb onto my lap, which melted my heart. All this frustration and then she does something amazing such as using her body to get her to move to a place she wanted to be at. And she is wanting a lot more cuddles on my lap too, as she feels safe there.

I thought it would be a good time to try her for a bedtime wee, but when she sees me put on my coat (it's freezing outside!), she gets all excited. This time, although I was just three paces away from her, she rolled off the sofa, landed on her feet and was trying to move to me - this was two seconds! She was all ok, but didn't wee when I took her out. The final time taking her out, I was just so frustrated as she wasn't holding any weight, she was just curved around to the right and no amount of straightening her – whilst holding her body weight – worked and she didn't wee. This, I can say, is the hardest part. She squeals to go out but only actually toilets for one in six attempts. But each attempt I have to carry her, and then support her, so it's physically demanding on my back, as well as cold, and I need the headtorch when it's dark, which is early now. I admit I was speaking to her very frustrated – not shouting, but totally fed-up type volume. I gave her a hug after. It's not her fault.

It was another disturbed night, as every time she moves on my bed, I worry that she will fling herself to the edge and fall off, so, I woke up loads.

Friday 29th November

Exhausted again after last night. We had another McTimoney booked for the morning, this is at home. She is mainly having massage but also checking her spine alignment (not near the neck area), and releasing tension, especially as she is banana-ing and tense on one side. She enjoyed it, despite a mid-session poo in her bed! The therapist also noticed the difference in how Reba is holding herself.

More trips outside (for nothing), she is snoozing between, whimpering at other times and this seems to be our days.

We ended up going to bed late as I took her out three times, but no toileting – this is important for what happened in the night!

Saturday 30th November

Oh, what a night. We didn't have the best sleep the night before, so this time I let her on my bed whilst I read a little bit, but then put her in her bed to sleep. She had a Trazadone (I swear they have less effect on her now) and as soon as I got in mine and switched off the light, I heard some squeaks and a thud, so back on with the light, got up, walked around the bed and had to lift Reba back in as she had tried to crawl out. Back into bed, light out, 30 seconds later... thud. So again, light on, put her back into her bed, and then back to mine. Each time she moved or made a hint of a noise, I told her 'go to sleep' – an old cue of ours. Well, it worked... for a bit! About 1 a.m., squeaks, and a thud. Light on, sort out Reba by lifting her back into bed, back into mine, light off, and about 15 seconds this time, thud. Here we go again! Finally, both of us in bed, light off and sleep... till about 2 a.m. Lots more noise and movement, go to investigate and she's weed in the bed. I use the washable pee pads so lifted her out, took out the pad, had the other one on my bed (for when she was sleeping there), then she was a bit damp so went downstairs to find the waterless foaming shampoo and a towel. Gave her a quick clean and dry, and back to bed we both went, but literally as soon as I switched the light off, thud... OMG! Got her sorted again, and this time managed to get back to sleep – till about 4.30 a.m. and it all happened again, till 7 a.m., and then 9 a.m., when I gave up. She was quiet for my quick shower but when I went to pick her up, there was poo nuggets in the bed. Thankfully she had not squished them.

She was not interested in breakfast but eventually ate it all slowly. Then, harness on to help me hold her, took her out and nothing. Tried again 30 mins later, nothing, but this time she wasn't even putting her back legs down. Literally collapsing on me. I must admit, I was frustrated and raised my voice a bit, as I'm in pain with my back from bending over holding her. And her not taking any weight is even more painful for me, as well as super annoying that she isn't even holding her legs vertically down but bringing them up under her belly.

I had an online consult at 11 a.m., and she was whining non-stop in her bed next to me. Took her out twice in the next hour after and she hadn't toileted. What little routine we did have is out of the window, and this is even more intolerable for me.

Today I just want to cry.

I'm tired, so frustrated, so annoyed, fed-up with the accidents when I take her out so often and really angry she isn't even trying today with holding her weight.

When she is upright, she bends strongly like a lower case 'r', so her left front constantly knuckles over, and she lifts her left hind off, so it's not taking any weight, but this leg is the worst anyway and doesn't hold in the right position. I've been told to keep her straight (impossible with holding her up, holding her legs and trying to use my knees to stop her shoulders turning) and she won't lie on the other side as she instantly turns over.

I don't know what more I'm supposed to do, certainly as being on my own with her.

I'm struggling, emotional and it's only lunchtime.

The afternoon was a bit better, we just relaxed. I took her out lots, she did two wees, but no bedtime wee...

Still totally shattered.

Forgot to give her the trazadone before bed, but as we went upstairs, I thought I would see how she went.

First off, she dozed on my bed as I read my book, but once I put her down to her bed, and switched off the light, it was carnage.

What I could hear was a squeaky pulse, like a fast heartbeat. It was just below a voluminous whine, but constantly there, interspersed

ONE PAW AT A TIME

by her licking lips and gulping. Whatever I said did nothing, but the whines escalated to panting. And of course, her trying to move and landing half out of the bed.

Quite a few attempts, some literally just as I switched off the light. I even brought up the bed from downstairs, as it is slightly bigger and a bit more room to stretch out her legs but that made no difference.

I was sitting on the side of my bed, almost asleep as whenever I moved into bed she panicked.

It's just too risky now to have her on the bed in case she moves and falls off, and she's been having accidents in the night too. Can't afford a new duvet!

Eventually I went down to get her tablet, wrapped in ham and gave that to her but it takes a while to take effect, so the next 30 mins were torture, with her panting and whining, and me struggling to not collapse. Eventually, I managed to slide myself into bed and voila, sleep. Well, until 6 a.m. when some grunting woke me up - she had wet the bed. So I stripped off the pee pad, put her in the other one (as we had two upstairs at this point), quick foam shampoo on her back end, and thankfully she went back to sleep. Bliss at last.

Sunday 1st December

Woke up at 10 a.m.!

I am totally convinced that she is scared of the dark now, so have had to order a nightlight. Now, I need it dark to sleep, but she is scared so this will be an interesting combo! Found a dimmable one so will see what that does.

Also ordered a new dog bed (it's Black Friday deals) as the one she has was always used upstairs – eight years old, no chew marks, and has had new memory foam mattress replacements a few times – doesn't allow her to stretch out, and her hind left leg is quite rigid and sticks out when she sleeps. She doesn't bend it much, unless you put her upright and try to get her to stand on it, then it does bend up under her, so no weight is on it!

I never thought I would be needing to change her bed, as a larger one won't fit in my small bedroom, but these are exceptional times and thankfully there are a lot of discounts out there this weekend. The new one only has three sides, so she has a pillow but can flick out her legs without anything in the way, and I hope this is comfy for her.

It's raining this morning, and despite two trips so far, no toileting. She is not so enthusiastic for her breakfast, but this could be linked to the meds and the lack of exercise/stimulation. She is likely stressed/depressed a bit too, as it must be so hard not understanding why she can't get up and walk.

I might try a snuffle mat whilst doing the physio today, see if that works.

Well, I videoed the snuffle/physio combo. She was so manic for the snuffle, that it was quite hard work as she was straining forwards!

When I placed her on her 'off' side, she sat up mid-way to hurl herself around so managed to get her to 'wait', took a pic, and grabbed the squeezy cheese to get her to turn to the left. Yes!!

Picked her up, as she is more upright, but still likes to flop her head on my shoulder, and she headbutted my eye socket. The bruise was hidden by my shadows under my eyes!

We had four nighttime wee attempts - nothing!

At bedtime, she twice had to be put back into bed after putting the light out within three mins, as she gets her front out and then gets stuck or rolls right out – one time I knew, as my bed vibrated as she hit it! There's not much space in my bedroom!

1.30 a.m. heard squeaks, managed to get her outside for a wee – headtorch, dressing gown and holding a peeing dog!

More squeaks and a thud at 6 a.m., as she had done a very small poo but didn't want to lie in it.

ONE PAW AT A TIME

Monday 2nd December

Another broken night's sleep. Tired, very achy, sore back and shoulder today.

Quiet morning, a few toilet attempts before success, and some standing practice, then she snoozed until it was time for her weekly hydro session. She did more straight laps to help her keep straight, and that worked, and she was trying to take steps when they stood her on the pod. As long as she is fighting to move, then she is more than likely to make progress.

I took advantage of a sleepy dog in the car, to run into the supermarket to get a basket of essentials – milk, bread, yoghurts and biscuits, oh and some mince pies!

Someone sent a message saying that I'm doing amazing, and Reba is lucky to have me. I know this but this still makes me emotional to hear.

At hydro, whilst chatting with receptionists, there was a pug that is permanently disabled on both rear legs, and has a weekly swim (brought to the practice by the housekeeper). He has wheels but owners have accepted the fact and do their best to give him a great life. They said that I was also special as I never gave up on Reba, as many would have opted to put their dog down with situations such as ours, but that also what happened to Reba was so rare, they have never heard of such an accident happening.

Was hoping for a quiet night – oh I can dream!

She was all cosy on my bed, but as soon as I moved her to hers, and switched off the light, it was chaos. She moved off the bed almost instantly, so had to lift her back on. Barely got the cover back over myself and 'thud', here we go again. Then she was squeaking so ran downstairs with her, but as I had to stop to put a coat on, she had already pood on the floor in the kitchen, and on the way out of the door. Back upstairs, and thud, she had moved off the bed again. I was thinking that I may need to swap this new three-sided bed with the one

I have been using downstairs that is four sides (no lower point on it), and a little bigger so she has room to stretch her legs, as the left ones don't curl up as much anymore. Anyway, there is a lot of scrabbling from her and then the smell hits me, she's wet the bed (there's always a double layer of pads on it). I clean it up, then realise the shampoo is downstairs so go back down to get it, so I can clean up her damp leg, and back to bed for me. Within seconds, she's off the bed again, so off I go downstairs to swap the beds over. Finally, there is peace, and I think 'yes, she's been to the loo now so I can have a good night's sleep', it's only been 20 mins since we went to bed, and all this has already happened.

Well, 5 a.m. and there are more scrabbling sounds. She flicks both her back legs together to move, think dolphin tail movement, but without the grace or effectiveness! Check on her and she's wet the bed again. Another clear up and back to sleep.

Tuesday 3rd December

I woke up about 9.30 a.m. shattered! Have a call at 10 a.m. so a quick dress and breakfast. Reba did another big wee (very strange) and then lay on my lap for the call.

At lunch, she did another big wee, and now I'm getting concerned. Decide to take her out to town as I need to visit the bank, so we arrive, walk by the river with her in her buggy, pop into the bank, and then on the way back through the town, decide to treat myself to a coffee. Find a chair where I can park the buggy next to me without blocking access, and the lady on the table adjacent to me (other side of Reba) starts talking. Most people do ask about her in the buggy, so quite used to it but she had finished her drink and food and so I thought she may then leave. But no, she seemed lonely, as she talked at length to me, without taking a break, and some quite detailed medical stories. Reba got very restless, so I made my excuses to leave (and certainly before any more family member death stories happened) but as I got to the car, I saw that Reba had wet herself.

Once home, she weed again so called at the local vets as the pee on the pad was stained.

With the help of a few of us, they managed to express her and got a sample – there was a lot of wee again! It was confirmed she has a UTI, so she is on more medication to help her.

The dimmer light finally arrived, and I plugged that into the bedroom. She is still on trazadone but once she got used to, it was much better, she thankfully stayed dry, but she didn't try to get out of bed and slept well. When she did move, I could make her out faintly so could see if she needed my help or not, and for most of the night, she didn't. However, I'm on tenterhooks, as each time she moves, I wake up. My cortisol must be through the roof.

Wednesday 4th December

Reba only had about half her breakfast – thankfully including the sweet potato hiding her tablets – and she is only having half portions now, she is just not eating as much. She has lost weight, just over a kilo, so now about 10.5kg. This is due to her reduced appetite, not moving around and so has some muscle wastage. This is close to her old steady weight of 10kg, it was only after COVID that she went to 11.8kg. A tiny bit lighter for me to hold her, but it doesn't feel like it as I still hurt lifting her!

She slept till after lunch, poor baby, literally passed out and not a flicker from her. No toileting, so hopefully the meds are doing their magic and healing her UTI.

I had a delivery, and the paper packing was interesting, so I found a shallow box, scrunched the packing paper in it, and dropped some treats in. The plan was to put the box down about 4ft from Reba, then turn around, pick her up, place her near and sort her feet out whilst she snuffled around for them. As with all best laid plans... they failed! As I put the box down, she leapt up and literally took a few steps to the box before I even had a chance to reach down for her! She was so excited, she was frantically sniffing for the food. Not the calm enrichment I was anticipating.

I was so stunned, and very impressed. She couldn't stay balanced or on her feet, so I straight away grabbed the handle on her harness and let her enjoy the treat finding.

I wanted to record it, so I set up the camera and repeated exactly – Reba obliged and did the same! Her left feet were sliding under her as she was snuffling around, so I was having to adjust regularly, and then when it was done, she took some steps away!

She's not good with knowing when she needs the toilet, it has regressed sadly, but I hope it improves again.

We just chilled in the evening, and then at bedtime, she stayed in the bed (thank you, night light and trazadone – although the effect of that is not as strong as before). But at 1.30 a.m. she was scrabbling around and had wet the bed, so cleaned it all up, new covers on, but she was again messing about at 5 a.m. Another cover change, and I had to get a third cover from downstairs for her bed to manage till we got up.

She was quite fidgety, so I didn't get much sleep.

Thursday 5th December

I had to set the alarm this morning as had an earlier (to normal) call – I struggle so much in the mornings, as I've never had a good night's sleep. Even though this was 9.30 a.m., it was a rush to get showered, dressed and feed Reba before the call. Didn't really get breakfast, and Reba barely ate hers (managed to get the pills down).

At the start of the call, she was mithering so picked her up and as I put her on my lap in front of the live Zoom call, she pooped!

A local trainer came over to help, and Reba did an excited poo for the new visitor! She doesn't even realise it is happening, poor girl. She helped with the physio exercises and really understood why I can't do all of them on my own!

Reba was moving around, climbing on me, launching herself around and they were surprised about how mobile she is and so relatively soon after her op.

Reba slept for the afternoon, then as the rain started, it was the battle for the toileting!

I actually prepped her dinner and placed on the floor for the first time so I could hold her up to eat as dogs would normally. She enjoyed that.

In the evening, I caught her shifting around on the sofa next to me, a signal she may need the toilet. As I stood up and went to get my raincoat on, she was barking. I looked around and she was on the floor! She had tried to jump off the sofa, but a splat landing. I won't be telling the physios or vets about that – again!

I've washed all her covers, so we have three on standby for tonight's dramas.

Before bed, she was shuffling around next to me, and ended up lying on her belly but had pushed her bum in the air, so was using her back legs to do this.

We tried a few times again for a bedtime wee, to no avail.

Quite a disturbed night, she woke me about 1.30 a.m., and then again more at 4 a.m. where she had wet the bed. She scrabbles around to push the wet pee pad to one side, and it is this movement that wakes me. She decided then to not let me sleep, but I can't be too cross as I could see her in the light of the nightlight literally circling around but with her full body off the ground horizontally. I couldn't see where her left legs were placed, or which direction her paws were (knuckling or not). Eventually managed to get her to settle about 5 a.m., when we both fell asleep until 8 a.m. which still felt too early!

Friday 6th December

Had a client consult, and quite quickly at the start, Reba moaned until she was on my lap, where she snoozed for most of it. Well, until I noticed a small puddle by my foot! It think it was the way her rear legs were stretched forward across my lap with her bottom sticking out, so a small leakage. Put her on the mat behind me, and she was quite happy there until the end of my consult.

We had planned to go to the lake but couldn't park so we went on into our local town and pushed the buggy around the pet shop for a treat. It wasn't until the afternoon when we got back that she finally had a wee.

I'm so tired today, and even forgot to offer her a drink regularly, which is not good for her waterworks.

Getting low on food, so need to plan an online shop, but I miss browsing the shop to select it myself. It's these 'normal' things that can't happen right now.

We had a rough night, she was awake at 1 a.m. and 3 a.m., and the noise of her fidgeting on the pee pad is so noisy. I eventually moved it off her bed and she finally went to sleep again about 4 a.m. and I was praying for a dry night too.

Saturday 7th December

We had a really stormy day today, loads of rain so it was quite miserable for both of us to go out in the garden for her toileting. It's very windy too, not fun!

I have Reba booked into her first groom since the accident this afternoon, and just hope all the roads are clear and no fallen trees. I don't like driving in these conditions, but she needs a clean and I need help doing it. If all we can do is a bath and nail trim, then I will be happy, and anything else is a bonus.

I chatted to our groomer beforehand, and as I have insurance for working with animals, she has agreed that I can be her assistant and help. I will need the buggy as although not far from the car park, it's over two roads, up a hill and too far to carry the heavy lump!

Arrived at the groomers and she could see that Reba had some ability to take weight on her front legs (if we straighten out the left paw each time she moves), but she is wobbly on her hind legs as her legs slide under her as her hips roll to the side.

In the washtub, she found two padded slings that we placed under her chest and waist. I also held her in place and helped shampoo. Next, she was on the table to dry, and our groomer set up both blowers so we both could get her dry quicker, and both could support the end we were holding. It wasn't worth moving her to the other table, as she was still in the two padded slings and so it was easier for her to bring her clippers over. I did have lots of treats on me as well to help Reba have a better experience, which came in handy as she was not happy with her nails being done but she did tolerate a full body clip - amazing! I said that I wasn't looking for neat or tidy, just anything is better than nothing so we were both pleasantly surprised by how much Reba could do.

It was then back in the buggy, with the hood down (Reba insisted on sticking her nose out of the corner) and fighting the elements to get back to the car. She was super tired but at least lovely and clean again. This was the first bath since her accident.

Sadly, the tiredness didn't translate to a good night, as she had me up every two hours, with a 4 a.m. pee all over herself and the bed.

Sunday 8th December

Woke up, fence panels blown down after another stormy night – more bloody expense!

She just didn't wee today till much later in the afternoon, which stresses me, and it means I'm carrying her out often, standing over her holding her up, all for nothing to only try again a little later, and again, and again.

I feel pressure to make 'visit dates' from family, and to 'do Christmas pressies' despite me saying I'm not bothering, can't afford it, and wont expect anything, as I can't do anything back – already been told there are some so that is really making me angry and upset, and crying, as I can't cope with this extra pressure.

Nighttime toilet – when I moved on sofa she indicated (like she used to) and did a poo but nothing else. Then she wet the bed about an hour after our last effort, and had gone to sleep.

For the rest of the night, she has been standing up and scrabbling around every two hours, so a really disturbed night.

Monday 9th December

At today's McTimoney massage, she showed she could get up, tried to stand on her back legs to climb up on me (I was sitting on a chair at the time), but she relaxed much more into the treatment this time. And less adjustments needed on her spine, she particularly liked the front right massaged, as that is taking so much more of the strain and weight.

Took a video of her eating her dinner – standing up! She had her harness on but managed to move my hands totally away for about a minute and she was balancing!

Spoke to vets about nighttime meds, they suggested she can have two trazadone (as well as the last of the meds from the UTI as one is a 24hr painkiller). Let's hope.

Tuesday 10th December

Well, that didn't work.

She still woke up every two hours (longest stretch), wet the bed, a little poo just outside of the bed in the morning as well. It's not just a quick shift/move position but she is getting up on all four paws, scrabbling around for ages. The noise of the pee pad being scratched is waking me up, but really she wasn't like this before, maybe once in the night, but not every few hours. When I switch the light off (both at the start and after the clean-up), she is visibly trembling. Without the trazadone, she escalates to panting and more.

We are ruling out pain with the vets, but this could be behaviour (PTSD?) as scared of the dark, but the lack of sleep is killing me, and probably her. At least she can nap during the day.

I had her standing for breakfast, as she was not so interested lying down eating it. I thought that if I could, I would try and put her harness on standing up as that would be so much easier, so I reached back for it as it was on the counter behind me. The clips made a noise as I moved it, she startled, fell down and rolled over her bowl and ended up on the other side of her bowl but standing up! (I only had one hand near her and couldn't catch her). I had to only straighten the one front left paw, but she was standing up of her own accord! Reset her to her breakfast and she stayed upright whilst I put on her harness.

Was really surprised! Very impressed! Just not on video...!

We tried a bit of scent detection work. I set up a tiny piece of Kong in the large tins and held her up so she could sniff each one. They were very close to each other so she didn't need to move much, but she was desperate to do this! I gave her treats for each success, and she was a bit rusty, but we had a few goes and she loved it. Hid a tiny bit in the kitchen cupboards at nose level and held her as she moved around to find it. She was sniffing lovely and found it, so very rewarding for her. But killed my back! Set up a stuffed feeder toy on her bed to finish off.

Later that evening, she gave me a five to eight sec warning, and this was a poo! We finally had a warning, even if I only made it to the kitchen. This feels like I'm writing the toilet diaries! But this element is so tiring, draining and important to me.

She eventually had a wee late afternoon, and after three attempts, she finally had a nighttime wee about 11 p.m., so I was quite happy to feel that she won't be likely to wet the bed and may settle...

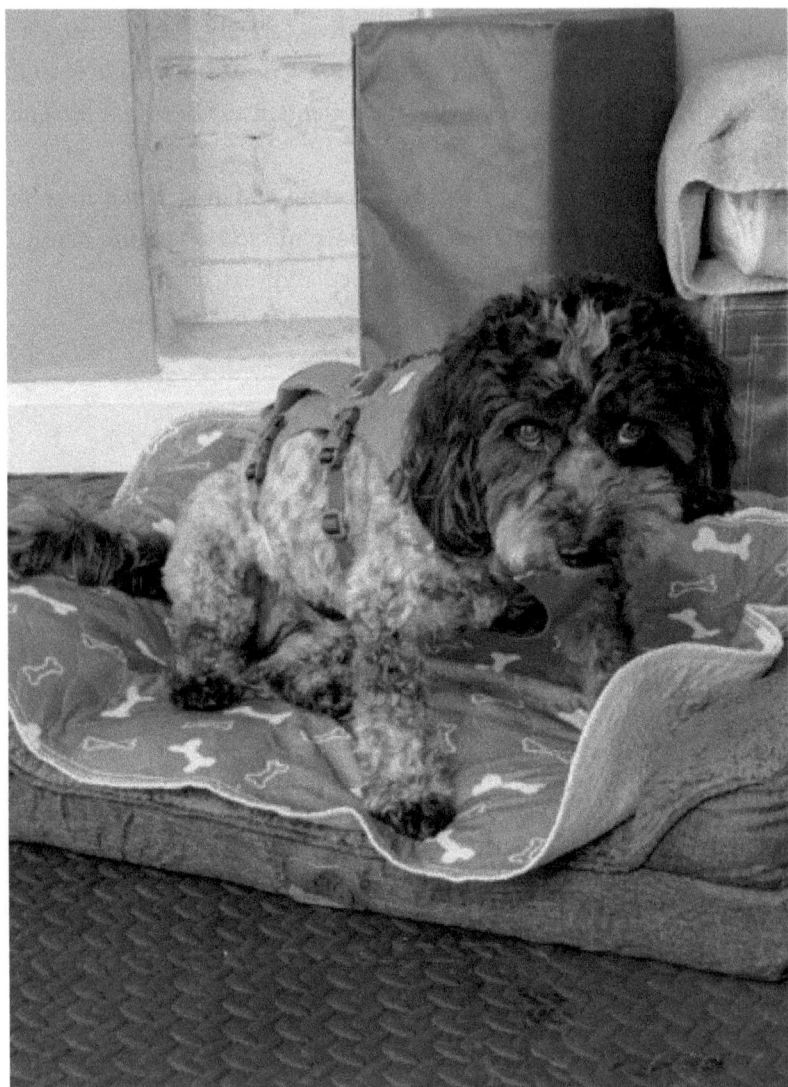

Wednesday 11th December

She settled on my bed, but within 10 mins of her being in her own bed and the light off, she was scrabbling around, disturbed. Despite going to her, talking to her and trying to settle her, she was on and off for a few hours but eventually settled about 2 a.m., where she stayed quiet and I managed to sleep uninterrupted till 8 a.m.! Still shattered, huge shadows under my eyes and fatigued.

No toileting this morning, but she gave me a five sec warning for a poo just before we were about to leave for hydro.

She didn't do as well today. Still 12 lengths, and they doubled up before a rest. During the rest she was extending her front left, but didn't move it during the swimming part. They managed to get a bit of movement at the end, but it appeared she was tired. I bundled her under blankets whilst I quickly collected my supermarket shop (it was already picked, so it only needed loading into the car).

Need to keep practising extending the legs for the physio. She is practising balancing when she is standing, mainly on the grass whilst I wait for her to decide to toilet or not.

Again, we had a bedtime wee, but this time she was agitated for at least two hours continuously after the light went out. She was only about 3ft from the dimmer switch and her silhouette was on the radiator behind her so I could easily see from my bed if she was lying down or not. Eventually she settled, and I had a long sleep. Two nights in a row! But it's a late night so not that rested.

Thursday 12th December

Got up about 9 a.m., was really not wanting to this morning! After breakfast, I drove to the vets to pick up her new meds – they are suggesting Sileo Gel at night instead of the two trazadone. We will see how that helps tonight – scary!

She's very tired today, sleeping a lot so I might have to wake her to get her active. It's damp and cold outside, and getting dark early so no walk today, but will plan something tomorrow as we will have a free day.

Once again, she did a nighttime toilet, so that was one worry off the list. The new meds (very expensive at £45) were tried tonight. Gave her some of the gel just before we went up to bed.

Lifting her off my bed after a few minutes, she was so settled and quite floppy, which did send a shiver down my spine as the last time she was like that was THAT night. Within minutes of turning off the lights, she was whining and crying, and shuffling a bit. This went on for about 30 mins, before she settled. However, the gel is not long lasting, so by 1.30 a.m., it was a nightmare. She escalated by also repeatedly getting out of bed, trying to walk and falling over as well as the crying. By 2.30 a.m. I'd had enough, and gave her another dose. This worked and we both slept for about three hours but then it was constant moving, whining and crying non-stop. Nothing I could do (apart from sit on my bed and stroke her) stopped her.

Friday 13th December

Woke up crying. Literally. Just didn't want to get up. It's super early, Reba is distressed, and I'm broken.

She's still whining after breakfast, and to be honest, it was like this all day.

Just keep crying today, I can't deal with this fatigue anymore. I'm stressing about the lack of income and paying for expensive meds that don't work, I'm at my wits end.

We went for a different walk, but the path was bumpier than I remembered, and the hill was steeper, so we never made it to the lake, it was some effort to get back up!

On the plus side, she is quite often shifting to her belly, and pushing herself up, back end first. The front left is mostly knuckled so she is not level, but it did make me smile that she stood up, tried to do a shake and fell over.

Vets phoned in the evening after my frantic message to them, and I was still upset and crying. They said the gel for some dogs knock them out for 12 hours! Not my girl. After a chat, they decided to go back to a gabapentin/trazadone combo to see if that works.

Saturday 14th December

Well, apart from some barking as a little poo nugget had escaped and she didn't want to lie in it, we had the best night since the accident. Both of us slept. I still feel very fatigued and not very refreshed, but I do feel better than I did yesterday.

Just a relaxing morning, and a bit of her physio.

With all meds, it often is a trial to find the right one, the right dose, changing doses, and even then, trying combinations. Maybe we have found one that finally works! I'm hoping.

Had a friend visitor, so we talked dogs for a while. Reba wanted to crawl on my lap, I was sat on the floor with my legs out in front of me. She had her front paws between my legs, her bum and back legs hanging behind, when she suddenly leapt and ended with all four legs on the far side, such a leap – and witnessed! My friend was very impressed with how much stronger Reba is.

Meds were a bit later tonight, so after we had a cuddle and I read for a bit. when I put her down, she was very alert and wouldn't put her head down. Every time I went to her, she was trembling a bit. She woke me at 1.30, 2.30 and 3.30 – one was a poo alert, the rest she was just juddering.

Sunday 15th December

Went for a walk with the buggy, only a short stroll in Blackheath but we cut through the woods and on the edge of the heath to the other car park where the coffee cart was. Not seen the lady there for a few months, and she was quite shocked to see me rock up with Reba in a buggy! But we stopped for a chat and a drink, and Reba had lots of attention from the customers there, as well as some dogs going to sniff her, so this was all good for her.

Mum came over later for lunch with some food, some Christmas presents for me, and a chat. She could see just how much Reba had improved too, which was lovely to know.

Made sure meds were a good hour before bedtime, and Reba was very snoozy on my bed whilst I read. So much so, she was part curled up and dreaming. Her movements during sleep are more erratic and unpredictable, and this was the case as in her dream, she jerked, bounced up in the air and turned 180 degrees, and again in the next second – I quickly saw she was then having a surprise poo, so managed to slide her back onto the pad (which is always on my bed when she is up there) so that my duvet was saved! Cleaned up and let her settle again. Once I put her in her bed, she stayed quiet and sleeping till I got up at 8.30 a.m. A fantastic night's sleep. There had been one more nugget in the corner of the bed, but otherwise a perfect night for a change!

Monday 16th December

Despite the good sleep, I don't feel refreshed, I think it will take a while before I do.

Deciding whether to go out for a walk or not today. We've a busy week of appointments but it's cold out there, and it's physically hard for me with the lifting of the buggy, pushing it and lifting her. My back is really taking the strain which is not great.

Nighttime, she woke up about every half hour between 1 a.m. and 3 a.m. so quite disturbed night but after that it was all good.

Tuesday 17th December

No breakfast allowed for Reba, so I kept mine to a minimum as we had to get her check-up CT scan done at the referral centre today.

They scooped her out of my arms and took her through to prep for sedation, and I was told to come back in an hour. I showed the surgeon a video of her standing up by herself, and they seemed impressed.

Snuck in a quick supermarket shop – just a basket as not really time to do more. But that was still a treat, having a little look around for things.

Came back an hour later, and they had a very sleepy puppy! I was asked to wait to chat to the surgeon, but was told the X-Rays were all clear – so nothing had moved internally and all bones healing well.

Ended up with a very dozy Reba asleep on my lap in the waiting room for over an hour (the surgeon was busy with consults), and then we had a quick chat. He recommended a session with the senior physio for some very specific exercises for her front wrist which has very little strength in it. He adores Reba, saying he forgot how cute she was and was kissing her head!

Reba was totally zonked out all day, snoozing, and barely doing anything. Hardly wanted a drink but did eat her dinner. No toileting.

At night, she was calm for the start but as soon as the light was out, she was whining. Instead of a regular breath, she almost 'catches' her breath so really quick, short ones, with a whine on the exhale with her mouth closed, so more like a squeak.

This was continuous, I just couldn't settle her. After two hours, I finally fell asleep but woke 90 min later to her whining and squeaking. This carried on for another two hours or so before she finally went quiet and slept, so I did too.

Wednesday 18th December

She's still lethargic, and not really using her left hind leg whereas before it was doing much better. Still not toileted. She's very subdued. No idea what sedation they used but she's still knocked out!! Now it's worrying. She's juddering as she breathes too.

She's also not putting her rear left leg down, and if it is, then it's knuckled. This is such a shock as this leg had been doing better.

Finally, about 2 p.m., she did a wee! Phew! It's been 48 hours since a poo but hey, one thing at a time.

I sprinkled some treats on the mat indoors and held her up to get her using her legs. Well, not quite a success as she was just dropping her hips, so when I took her out to the garden, I let her lunge forward and placed her legs as best I could. She started to 'walk' her back left, even if it was knuckling a bit, but there is no attempt to bring her front left forward yet. Let's hope the physio, hydro and massage this week triggers some nerve stimulation here.

Today's regressions have got me quite emotional, partly due to the lack of sleep but also some frustration that this has happened and sad, too, for her future. I really want that front leg to start moving forward unaided... this will be the start of a gamechanger for us – allowing her to move more independently, able to stay balanced and not topple forward, but in future able to get on/off furniture and the bed, then she may sleep better if she is safe to do so. Happy to give up a bit of my bed as a compromise if that helps her PTSD and fear of the dark/nights.

Well, she started to use her hind left more in the evening, and did another bedtime wee.

Tough night. Despite all her meds, she was squeaking lots. Just wouldn't settle. It started about 12.30 a.m. and went on and on. Got up several times but mostly was just kept awake by her. Grabbed a bit of sleep here and there, but at 5 a.m. I woke to a thud, and then saw her stumbling/ walking out of the bedroom and across our short hallway. Thank goodness I have a staircate across the top otherwise she would be tumbling down it. There was a trail of nuggets, the first poo since Monday! Cleaned up, settled her back down, and was secretly pleased with her, which lasted about two mins before she started whining again.

Thursday 19th December

Shattered once more. She was mithering so grabbed my jogger bottoms and dressing gown and took her out. She did another poo – but this time she actually started to round her back – a proper squat!

Took a while to prompt her to eat breakfast, then managed to sneak upstairs for a shower. She only barked once.

As soon as I was back downstairs, she needed taking out again and this poo was not looking like her normal nuggets – yuck! She must be back to normal now after the sedation, so must remember this for the few days after her next scan in six weeks.

She had both a physio consult (super expensive!) and hydro today. We have some more exercises to help stimulate her nerves in her pads, and more balance exercises. It's all very specific to help that front leg.

She did better in the hydro session too, and holding her weight when her rear right leg was lifted.

We've got lots of homework to do and need to get this sorted, as I can't afford much more professional help. Well, I can't afford any of this so far, but I will have to cut it at some point. I hope she improves enough to stop soon!

Came home, and as I was eating my late lunch, she was scrabbling on her bed but then did a wee – not her normal sign, and no notification or warning. Not so good. Her bowels are not happy after the sedation this week, four squidgy and smelly poos today alone.

Nighttime, not settled, and she woke often, mostly from 3 a.m. Whining, up and down, out of the bed lots, just a nightmare! It was so draining, that I felt that if got up to her one more time, I would be shouting in her face with frustration, which I certainly didn't want to do. I never want her to be scared or fear me, so I kept to my bed, and buried my head in the pillow, fighting back the tears, praying she will stop whining and let me sleep for just a few hours.

Friday 20th December

Her belly is still not right, and she was not very interested in breakfast at all. We had her McTimoney treatment and massage today. Reba was very excited, and the therapist saw just how much more she was moving. But she soon settled down and relaxed into the massage, enjoying the pampering. This is so good for keeping the muscles relaxed, especially those that are taking most of the weight, and for keeping the blood flowing to the not so good legs.

Too tired to go out today, the buggy is heavy lifting in and out of the car and the weather is grey and dull. Overall, a miserable day, feeling tired but we practiced lots of the exercises as well as the slicker brush on her paw pads. She did get a bit feisty – a great reaction, just what I wanted! I've been told to annoy her so I will, if it means a greater sensation to her feet.

Saturday 21st December

Breakthrough!

Not only is her belly better, but... she slept the WHOLE NIGHT! She got out of bed two minutes after the light went out, but after that, she slept!!! I woke up a few times myself, but Reba was snoozing happily!

Really windy outside, and where we can walk is so limited by the surfaces, so I just took her in the buggy around the village. No one around, nothing to see, I think everyone must be away or shopping!

It's the shortest day of the year, and with the cloud, it's a very dull, dark day too. In one respect, I wish she had hurt herself in the summer, as at least taking her out was warmer and drier (well, maybe not!) but the days are longer and so have more time to go out and about before darkness falls. I can't steer the buggy well in daylight, so would hate to try when I can't see where I'm going as clearly!

She was a bit unsettled at bedtime, but I was later in giving her the meds – I lost track of time! She woke at two, as there was a little nugget, but after that she slept through. Bliss!

Sunday 22nd December

There were two little dry nuggets in her bed that she had slept on! Kept her standing and doing some physio whilst she ate her breakfast, and then rested so I could get a chance to tidy up and catch up with some admin. There I am, trying to leave a voice note for instructions to a client for their training, and little madam behind me decides to get up to get a toy near her. She staggers up (her front left is still knuckled so she is lower on that side), grabs her toy and ends up walking in two circles (her right-side works, her left doesn't so going in circles is quite common!), then throws herself back onto her bed! Took me several goes to leave the message as I was laughing in the message and completely forgot what I was trying to say!

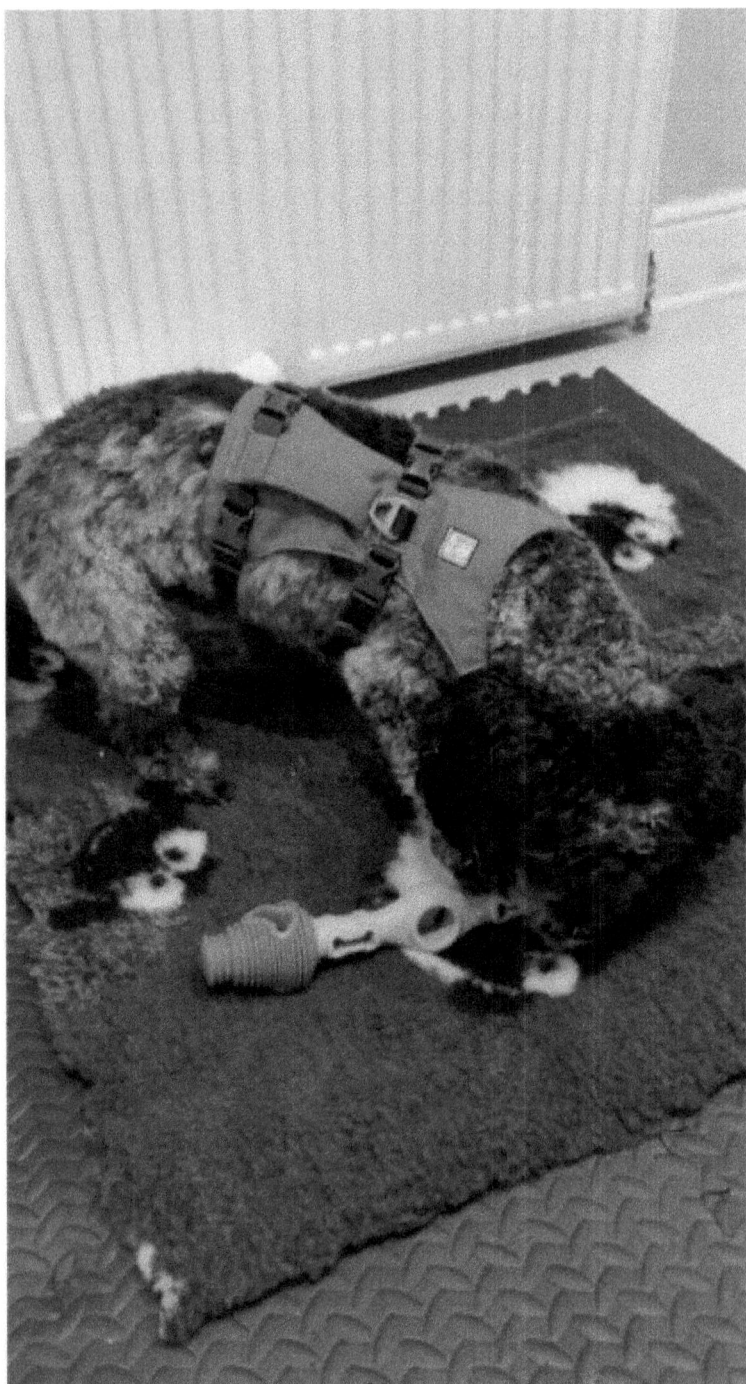

Monday 23rd December

Disturbed night again but had a chunk of sleep after her deciding to wake on the hour, every hour, from lights out till 4 a.m.! Then slept till 9 a.m. She is on a lot of sedation meds too, but oh no, they help reduce her anxiety about bedtime but not knock her out as they should!

We had hydro that afternoon, and it went well. I even heard them cheer at her! She was much better than two weeks ago, less lazy on her front leg (she realises she can still swim on three legs so won't use her fourth!). They worked her hard, sometimes even three lengths before the break, and even on the break, did a lot of posture work. By the end she was moving her front left with minimal prodding. This update brought me to tears, happy tears, as all I ask for is progress. As we were waiting our turn, the surgeon appeared as he was called into the physio area to help with another dog, and on the way out he saw us and came straight over to say hello and kiss Reba! I am being told her progress is slow, but she is an older dog, she won't heal as fast but to be honest, I think it's still amazing and she is making progress well.

Tried to get an early night, but her moving around wakes me, and she definitely needed her nuggets cleaned out at 5 a.m. and 6.30 a.m., but then managed to sleep after that.

Tuesday 24th December

Another trainer friend came over to help and brought a load of sniffing things -mats, platforms, surfaces to step on etc., and Reba had a lovely time with these, even if there were no treats. It was all the residual smells that got her fired up, and was very animated with the snuffle balls, so much so, she took them and was scampering away with them!

In between our tea and cake (yes, a pressie for me!), she helped with the physio exercises, mostly the sitting one. I struggle to do this as I need someone making sure the front legs stay put and correct, whilst I try and push Reba into a sit (I NEVER EVER use this way to move a dog in any other situation) whilst holding her legs tucked in for alignment. Reba has a big habit of splaying out her back right – the diagonal to the bad front left – so this needs to be kept in place and not out, meaning I need to use my legs and my hands to make sure she is in the tuck position. This is not yet a one-person exercise!!

Reba is now tired but keeps getting out of bed like a naughty toddler! Silently cursing but proud too! All this moving is great brain work, muscle work and good for her, but I'm not always close enough to keep righting her knuckled front paw.

I must be so used to waking up lots, as I was awake at 2 a.m., but then she woke about 3 and 4 a.m., and then I woke up at 6 and 8 a.m.!

Wednesday 25th December

Christmas Day!

Got up about 9 a.m. after a disturbed night. We cancelled all our plans, so we could relax and not be stressed about lively kids and chaotic households, and carpeted houses.

Our routine is that I get her breakfast and now make her stand up for it so she can practice balancing, placing her foot and some physio. Then I can grab some food for myself and take her out for toilet, as by that time she is ready (often if I try before, she won't go). So, today being a day of relaxation, she doesn't even wait for me to finish my breakfast before she shifts her fluffy butt off the bed (that has the pee pad on it), and starts a Niagara Falls wee on the vet bed (not waterproof!). No point disturbing her, so waited till she finished with the Urine Off spray at the ready, then scooped up the bedding and ran it up to the washing machine, after being dowsed in the enzymatic cleaner.

My back is super sore today, so I won't be going out in the buggy, but instead will just chill out together. Not much of an appetite, so skipped lunch but did cook a dinner.

Thursday 26th December

Wow, so last night she was grumbling whilst lying down in bed soon after I switched the light off, but I got up to do a quick stroke to settle her, then she slept the WHOLE NIGHT – and SO DID I!!! Our second full night's sleep since the accident! Not feeling refreshed but I really hope this continues! Said that last time!!!

No accidents in her bed, just a sleepy pup. Over the moon.

Decided to take her out without the buggy, just to get her to stand and move on other surfaces. I am hoping the new smells and people/dogs will motivate her. Recently, she will drive her back legs and try to run when I'm holding her harness on our lawn, as she now wants to choose the wee spot, but as soon as we get to the patio, or if we are out and I get her out of the buggy, she stands still, refusing to move.

The plan was the heath, but an unexpected closure of the rail crossing meant we went up to the outdoor café viewpoint. It was busy, but not so manic as it was foggy up there, and managed to park really close to the café area. It was closed, so only a few people milling around, but a few groups off for a walk. I took her to the seating area which is a mix of soft mud and small gravel pieces, before a concrete hardstanding area. I had on the belly support strap that the surgeons gave me, and clipped a lead onto the harness so I didn't have to bend down. Many dog walkers saw the straps and kept their lively bouncing dogs away. We didn't come across any calm ones, but I did get her moving a bit. I even managed to video some of her moving. She was bringing forward her back left, and there was some movement on her front but more often than not, it was knuckled, sometimes dragged a bit, but there were times it was extending forward and the paw was correct so really encouraging. We were out for about 10 mins, and she was tiring as her hips were drooping a bit, so we called it a day and went home for our coffee.

She is definitely wanting to move more, as she thought she heard the doorbell, and by the time I was at the door to check (no-one there), she had staggered to the kitchen/hallway doorframe.

When I put down her dinner, she was already out of bed and walking to it.

And then when I was about to start preparing mine, she was doing her urgent barking and was actually staggering to the back door! Her front left lets her down hence the staggering, and she stumbled to get around the last corner by the back door, but I was so impressed with her – after I scooped her up and took her out to wee.

Friday 27th December

Apart from some grizzling for the first hour, the night looked hopeful for sleep. Except, lots of moving around woke me about 6 a.m. and saw her rear leg cocked whilst lying down, and on closer inspection she had weed in the bed. Cleaned her up, shampooed her legs and thankfully she settled again, but I struggled to get back to sleep.

Went to visit my mum, so a very foggy drive and very on alert during our lunch. Had laid mats in the kitchen by the small table, so we stayed there as the floor was too slippery for Reba otherwise, and I dare not risk the carpeted areas! She did really well, getting up a few times, taking some steps too but mostly with her front left paw bent under so her weight was on her wrist. This is not good, but it's also impossible to keep righting it, it literally can be every few seconds. I think she found it very frustrating though, as normally she would be out exploring the garden or wandering around the other rooms, but instead she was trapped on a small island of pee pads.

I knew it had to happen – the poo in my slippers!

I swap from my (slide on) slippers to backdoor shoes in order to take her out the back door to toilet. At night, I stop to put on my headtorch, now one-handed!

She did her wee and as I tried to support her to 'walk' her back to the house, she stopped, as she has done before on reaching the patio stones. Picked her up under one arm, took her in, closed the door and was about to swap my shoes for my slippers when I heard a soft 'thud' or two. Looked down, and yes, there were three nuggets, but one had landed right in my slipper! Thankfully, they are normally hard and dry (her poos), so my slippers were salvageable.

A fairly quiet night, some grumbles but then she slept till about 5 a.m. when lots of moving around to get comfy – mostly to end up in the same position, but then she slept through till morning.

Saturday 28th December

She is coping well with the new raised feeding station I picked up yesterday. Last night, she jumped at the sound of the metal bowl on the metal frame, so this morning I weaved a ribbon around the holder, and bingo, she can now get up herself to get a drink and stand to eat.

Decided to take her out in the buggy and to go to our old regular haunt, the heath. It's a windy single-track road to get there, so often we take it slow as cars can suddenly appear. On the bend at the top of the hill, we had just turned past it when a car appeared, so I gently braked so I could reverse into the passing spot behind me. I wasn't going fast, but Reba is quite unstable! I have a big mirror in the boot angled down so I can see her in it from my rearview mirror. All I saw was her rolling along the small boot space, but she had managed to wrap the sandy coloured towel around her in the process so looked like a sausage roll! It was very funny! After that, she propped herself up into a sit in the corner of the caging and stayed like that for the final five-minute journey. As well as laughing all the way, I was also proud she was sitting up in the car.

No idea what position her front paw was in but still impressed.

She only had me up once in the night again.

Sunday 29th December

Just a quiet day today.

I managed to cue her into a sit, but as videoing it, I wasn't there to straighten her back feet, but it wasn't too bad. She's definitely getting better, but she holds her front left paw like an injury rather than using it. This really worries me, as until she can 'right' it, she can't walk. She won't go on any hard surface as it probably hurts her wrist, and I don't want her to get injured on the skin area with it dragging. We don't need that.

She was so annoying at bedtime. She often does the circling in the bed, but being super slow and wobbly, even she did about 20 turns which took an age, and I got quite frustrated with her. Eventually she did settle but I didn't after that!

Monday 30th December

We slept through! Well, she did, it took me about an hour to finally drop off but there were no interruptions! Sadly, it had to end as my alarm was set, needed to get up early as my car was being collected for repair by the garage, and of course, they turned up very late.

Could have had a full sleep as by lunchtime and several phone calls later, I was told the booking was a mistake and they won't be taking my car in today at all. Fuming! We had planned a day indoors and a visitor as we hadn't expected to have transport.

Reba was not too impressed to do her physio exercises, even though I had an extra pair of hands to help. We pressed on regardless with what she would do, as it's all very important.

Lazy afternoon, but at bedtime, within 15 mins of the light going out, she had wet her bed. Not had any accidents for a while, as she is now doing a nighttime wee. She is probably for some reason not fully emptying her bladder.

Tuesday 31st December

Hydrotherapy this morning, and whilst in the waiting room I showed the reception team how Reba can stand up still really well now. I normally just carry her in, she is then carried to the pool area and then carried back to my lap at the end, so they've not seen her progress despite seeing us weekly. They were super impressed! And she did better in the session, they could see her standing was much better, and she was using all four limbs to swim too. So happy!

Planning the evening so that she is not alone in her bed when the fireworks are due (even though they've been starting early). Meds and bedtime later than normal, so I'm reading at midnight and can reassure her. Even through her medicated state, she alerted and grumbled a bit but thankfully wasn't bothered.

Wednesday 1st January

Happyish new year!

Would be better if Reba could walk, but I will give her the time she needs to heal.

She is definitely more mobile, and as soon as I put her in her downstairs bed, by the time I've gone to my chair, she's already up and staggering towards me. She is hobbling around on three legs, her back legs splayed whilst her front left is over on her wrist. There are times when she is trying to place her left paw, and it's even the correct way round with pad down, but not often enough to enable her to walk properly or on harder surfaces.

Thursday 2nd January
She slept quite well, only a few stirrings in the night – which does always wake me, but she resettled and slept so that's still much better than before.

Lazy morning as later, we are getting a visit from one of her best friends. Byron and she met when they were only a few months old, and they get on so brilliantly. They will play a bit, but they are very respectful of each other too. His mum has become a really good friend, and she has popped over a few times over the last two months to see Reba. She was so upset at the news of her accident, as Reba has been to overnight stays often with Byron, and he comes here.

Wow, so they were both crazy excited to see each other! Reba was up and bouncing around, launching herself, falling over, and he was running around barking and so happy! We kept a close eye on them, gave them cuddles as Byron was very pleased to see me too, but not quite as much as seeing Reba! They eventually calmed a bit, and so we let them mooch about and then they started to initiate their play – they turn and back into the other one as an invite to start a gentle wrestle. To be fair, he was very gentle and when Reba fell over, he went down into a lying position to play gently with her. Lots of ear licks were happening and a bit of their pushing around, and they were so happy. There is so much joy to watch two dogs playing respectfully, and all the nuanced moves and body language that they communicate with each other too.

Byron is also very astute enough to stop when she does, so they both have a break from play and interactions if one of them needs it.

I'm sure this gave Reba a good mental boost as well as the neurological firing that her brain needs to be able to move. She was trying to place her foot too, and succeeded on a few occasions, brilliant. She rested well after that, but did wake up at 1 a.m. in the night.

Friday 3rd January

It's a very sunny but exceptionally cold day, and with horrible weather due again, decided to drive out to the nearest National Trust estate for a walk. There is a good, fairly level path that is stoned so better for buggies and a way around to avoid the fields and small hills/muddy areas. The car was so frozen that I couldn't open it for a while! It was a glorious walk, and I really enjoyed it. Reba was comfortable in the buggy, probably helped by the volunteers giving her biscuits at the entrance. It was not too busy, or muddy, as the path was still frosted over. My stamina is certainly awful at the moment, but my arm muscles are really strong from all the carrying her around!

Came back and our fencing guy is here to replace the panels that fell in the last storm. This is good as Reba is more active now, and at least the garden is secure again.

Saturday 4th January

Bitterly cold day, with a bit of snow due later (immediately followed by rain), so no plans to go outside for a walk. I took a video of Reba moving from her bed, across the room to where I was sat at the table. It shows the progress she has made, and the fact she doesn't want to stay in the bed and she can move around, but also really upset me about how she just wants to walk but cannot understand why she is unable to. She has one good strong leg, the front right, and so she leads with that. The front left is bent behind, and although I can sometimes see her shoulder moving and trying to bring the leg forward, it doesn't translate to her paw. But there is the occasional time the pad is facing down and she takes a 'true' step, but this is the minority. To compensate, as the legs work in a diagonal, the back right splays out more than it should, and 'stamps' so it fires up movement more often than it should. Her left rear leg is not quite there, as it is often hanging back and she is not great at bringing it forward, especially when she stops still. On top of all this, she moves forward with her body at a 45-degree angle, so moves like a crab. It takes her a lot of effort to move, and it breaks my heart to see her struggle so much.

Took her out for her bedtime wee, and there was a little spattering of snow, and she enjoyed shoving her nose in it, making little holes!

And apart from shuffling around about 30 mins after lights out, she slept all night, and so did I!

Sunday 5th January

Quite emotional today. Didn't wake up till nearly 10 a.m., as it was a rare night's sleep. Reba did a few poos as I picked her up, but almost expected it as not only does this happen most mornings, but we also were late getting up.

Wet day today, so no plans. We are kind of in a routine now, which is me trying to get motivated to start working again – social media creativity has passed me by, and my brain is still all over the place – and then doing her physio. She still doesn't even try and move from the ice cube on her paw pad, she doesn't even feel it. It saddens me, as I just want her to flinch, curl her toes, move her leg – anything, however small the movement.

When we have injuries, we understand, we learn to adapt, compromise, but we have the comprehension that we cannot move or do things the same as before. Dogs don't have the same awareness as us, and it is distressing to see her struggling and confused as to why she cannot move around as she has always done.

All I want is for her to be walking better. And that means her front leg healing to a better degree. Please...

Monday 6th January

Another night's sleep! I forgot to give her tablets last night till literally bedtime, but there was no panting or whining upstairs, or when I carried her into her bed. She moved a bit to resettle but then she slept through – brilliant for both of us!

We had hydrotherapy today, and they could still see an improvement. They made her swim 19 lengths, and could see more stability in her standing. It was noted that as time progresses, the rate of improvement does slow down, but she is still getting better from last week.

At home, when I sat at the table for a late lunch, she tried to run on the mats to me, so I recorded a few attempts at recall, as she had seemed to forget a lot of her cues. She was bouncing weirdly but came at speed at me! Very uncoordinated and dragging her leg, which makes her healthy back right leg mis-time too. I then slowly walked beside her to get her to walk slowly next to me, and we stopped every few paces and her front leg was placing a few times on that – recorded for proof!

I was hoping that she would be tired so I could do my online consultation call without interruptions, but I could hear her pottering behind me so ended up having her on my lap for the rest of the call, where she started to snooze. After, we had a cuddle for a while, and she then settled till dinner time.

Tuesday 7th January

Another great night, with only the usual early disruption as she tries to move the pee mat off her bed, with me replacing it and her doing her circles before settling, but we both slept well again. She is spitting out her trazadone and that is getting harder to give to her – last night I ended up breaking it open, spilling out the powder into a shallow dish and mixing it with squeezy cheese! It did the trick but not ideal...sneaky girl.

Her leg is not as good today, always on her wrist and dragging more, so I've been letting her rest with only bits of physio as the opportunity arises. She is, however, stumbling around the room, not really staying in one place.

I decided to try something, and that is to have her walk slowly by my side, with treats in hand, to see if that helps her placement. When on her own, she rarely rights it but what I did get (and videoed it), was when she was super slow, with her head up, more often than not she was placing her paw correctly, and all her legs were more coordinated than before. There's still lots of room for improvement, and she later went on to just slide her wrist when moving around after. But she can do it... just.

ANOTHER FIRST.... Before the accident, if I was prepping food, she would sit on the back door mat which is by the units, as I have given her treats there before. They never forget where they get fed! Anyway, tonight, when I was getting her dinner together, she made her way to the mat and sat there! I nearly cried! This is HER normal.

One thing that is new since the accident is the burping! After every meal, chew and treat. She never did before but now she's making up for nine years of never burping... really loudly too. Hilarious, but I hope it's not a symptom of something. It's not the speed of eating, as she has done it after lick mats, snuffle mats and small chews. Could be her new normal. Great, not!

Wednesday 8th January

It's freezing!!! We had to set the alarm as we were having a friend's dog over for a few hours today. Reba woke me about three times between 1 a.m. and 6 a.m., not just stirring but grumbling and barking. Shattered, and a little bit despondent as we have had a run of a few good nights' sleep too.

I've no batteries for the doorbell, it eats them up at such a rate, but the cost of an electrician is high as well. Maybe I need to get them in to do that and the new rear garden light. Must get some more quotes – the other guy was SO expensive for just the light. But now Reba is more mobile, I will be needing it soon. Right now, I can't risk her getting stuck under the bushes if she strays off the lawn, so need to hold her, and she won't walk on the patio section to get to the grass as it hurts her wrist.

Saturday 11th January

Despite her bedtime wees, she wet the bed at 1 a.m. She moved the pee pad out of the way and wet the cushion – the one thing I wanted to protect as this has been her bed since young, and the only one she has never chewed! She was huffing which made me get up, and glad I did! Apart from the odd early morning shuffling, she has pretty much slept most nights. Even when I'm late giving her meds, she is not distressed being upstairs now, so may even think about reducing her meds. I was going to consider removing the pee pad on her bed... not now!!

We've been without my car for the last few days as it went in for repair.

It's been sub-zero most days, so we've just been pootling around indoors, and doing her physio. Reba had her McTimoney yesterday and showed off her new moves. I've also booked some acupuncture for next week – expensive but need to get that front foot better as soon as I can.

Monday 13th January

I was needing to go to the supermarket, and as Reba has to wait in the car for me (she won't tolerate being alone, and not started the training to enable this yet) I was sat in the car with the heater on to warm it up, when our lovely post lady gave me some cards, and said that she had a package but it was in her van, and should she leave it by the bins. I then took Reba out, parked in the corner of the car park and raced around the shop. On getting home, I took her out in the garden so she could toilet. As she was stood there, I realised that I needed to check for the parcel, so turned my back and went through the gate – it was there! My back door is about two paces from the gate, so I went to put it indoors and Reba was still standing there. But as soon as I started to walk to her, she ran off to the side along the fence line, but there are huge shrubs in the way and my fear has always been that she will fall, get tangled and unable to get back up, and there is no way I can get to her.

Anyway, the cheeky monkey just stayed behind the shrubs! So, plan B is to go back and rattle the treat tin! Works 99% of the time! She popped out and I managed to get her to me so I could hold her for her toilet.

From now on, I will clip her lead on so she cannot run under the shrubs in the garden! But that also means I don't have to bend over holding her all the time, I can just hold the lead (she wears her harness all day now) and save my back by standing upright.

This is a huge step forward.

Later, she wanted to go out so clipped on the lead, stepped out, and where there is one step up about 1m from the back door, about one brick high so not much, but in her leaping uncoordinated way, she fell and where her legs were up against the upright of the step, got stuck! It didn't put her off and now she will mainly walk on the patio (well, her stumbling run) to the grass but not always go back so still need to carry her sometimes.

Sleeping is much better too, normally one early disturbance up to an hour after lights out, but then she will sleep through. Fantastic.

Tuesday 14th January

Visit to our local vet today for more meds, but I booked in to see the vet who was there THAT night. He had not seen her since then and was so impressed with her standing and walking a bit – the floor was a bit too slippery for her, but he still examined her and was super impressed with her progress so far. Yes, her left side is still affected but from when he last saw her, to now, is amazing. He was thinking about us a few days ago as he was walking his dog past my house (he lives in our village), so I think it was really nice for him to see Reba and just how far she has come. He also thinks a carpel support may help, and he's seen dogs with neuro damage learn to flick their front limb, so their pad lands the correct way for walking.

I was at home later having a cuppa and saw Reba shuffling to the back door – another huge milestone as she was not only indicating she needed the toilet but also made her own way to the door. Made me very happy!

Tonight, we are back at the vets but this time to see vet who will do her first acupuncture session.

Well, she did so well! She tolerated the needles, and the wait, so was a superstar! Now it's a case of let's see if or how this makes a difference. It fires up the nerves so it's not always obvious, but even a small change will help.

I gave her a reduced trazadone dose tonight, the start of her reduction of the meds. She was not distressed going to bed, but between 2 a.m. and 6 a.m. she got up four times, each time getting out of bed. Grrr! But will persevere.

Wednesday 15th January

My birthday! The best present would be her walking again, but she's still trying so that's enough for me for now.

What I have noticed is that sometimes, instead of her weight being all the way to her wrist when she knuckles, she has sometimes just had her toes knuckled, which is a noticeable change. She still does bend at the wrist a lot, but now we are progressing. I don't want her scuffing her skin, whether it be the wrist or the top of the foot, as an open wound will stop her completely, however I'm really happy that it is a change in the right direction.

Tonight, we were settled in front of the TV – yes, I know it's my birthday, but this is our rock and roll life right now!!! – and I totally forgot to get her meds. Took her upstairs, she snoozed next to me on my bed while I read my book and it was only when I carried her to her own bed that I realised! Ran downstairs, prepped her pills in her ham slices and thankfully she took them. Not sure what impact it has being so late, but she got out of bed a few times in the first hour, whenever I got myself comfy. Then I heard a thud, and there she was out of bed, standing next to mine. But I can't get annoyed as I could see she was standing perfectly! I just need her to do that during the daytime!

Thursday 16th January

She was quite lethargic and wobbly this morning, probably due to the very late meds last night.

We had double appointments today. First was the physio, and she was very impressed with the progress, and had some great ideas for exercises that will help with the front paw further. She had a carpel support so we tried it – it will either help the dog or make them drag their foot. Guess what happened with Reba – she was worse! She dragged her leg even more and was even lower on that side when standing. It can compromise the messaging from paw to brain if there is a gadget doing some of the work for it, so I'm pleased we could try it, but no, I won't be using one!

One thing she did comment on is just how tolerant Reba was when she was holding her paw up whilst fitting the support, and I said that she literally has been so good to allow anything and everything being done to her without any grumbling at all. Physio said she was very impressed with all the work I have done before this accident, to have such a lovely temperament in Reba. I did say that genetics played a part, I can't take all the credit!

Next, we moved to the pool for her hydro. The physio went in to watch for a bit too. The discussion after was that Reba is using all four limbs better, the loading through the left is better, so they want to try the water treadmill next time. It may not be suitable due to the drag of the water, but they want to try. Promotion! But also, more costly!

Physio is aware of my financial restrictions, but does want to see us again in four weeks but that is flexible depending on how Reba does.

Reba was sleeping in the car on the way home. It is exhausting, both physically and mentally, but she perked up at home. Even now, her paw is more correct than before, and only toes knuckling more often too. So pleased. She is standing better this afternoon since coming home too, her paw pad is down, and her back is level. Perfect!

Early meds tonight, but I struggled to sleep. About 1 a.m., just as I was finally thinking I could sleep, she got up! A few nudges and she went back to bed, but my brain was racing. Finally rested.

Friday 17th January

Start of our advanced rehab stage today!

We've new exercises to try, all designed to encourage more use of the front limb and stimulate the nerve pathway.

First off is the lie down to stand, with a lean forward so she can get used to the movement of her paw down and then the weight going through it. It doesn't matter if she lies down and it curls, as I need to straighten her foot before asking her to stand. She did about four reps – press ups are hard work, especially if you have been laying around for three months and not even walked! After the first one, she was sliding from a sit to a lie down but that kept her paws correct, so really good. One downside is the fact it made her unexpectedly poo! I think this was enough for now.

Next, I found my wobble cushion. It's a yoga rubber round but low, shallow, partially filled cushion, with bobbles on one side. I originally used it after I had knee surgery and needed to strengthen my balance and joint. Then I was using it for my puppy classes, where I set up differing objects to stand on and explore, as a confidence building exercise, but also using this wobble cushion helps body awareness and core strength, but the puppies were free to stand on it or not. Now it's coming in handy once again. Reba has to have her back legs slightly higher than her front to stand still, so there is more load/weight going through her front paws. I will also do the neck stretching, so keeping her feet still but making her stretch her head forward and sideways – using treats as encouragement, of course.

Reba did well, thankfully she is small enough to lift her back end to reposition herself, but she does like to spread her back legs wider than before for balance, and I need to check she keeps both paws on, and not sneakily remove one leg to the floor.

To also encourage using her front left, it was said to use chews and Kongs to get her to use it to stabilise the food or feeder toy. I tried the Toppl, the Kong, and a long-lasting chew – she was very happy to go paws free, or just her right paw to hold it but oh no, not any use of her left! She's too used to these and is crafty, she knows she can do it one-handed! On the plus side, it shows just how much range of movement she has in her neck, the pins and cement fusing her neck has no impact, in fact you would never know by the way she can tilt, turn and reach. It's only when you feel the underside of her neck and there is an uneven lump.

I was always aware of the neck biology. I can never remember the names of all things such as nerves, key blood vessels etc. which is why I would struggle in advanced behaviourist education, but I am certainly educated enough to understand impacts on the key structures. I mentioned at the vets earlier in the week about changes in Reba, and the fact she has started to burp loudly after eating each time. It's not a deal breaker, there are way more serious things to worry about, but it was just of note. They reckon that the new structures in Reba's neck may have shifted or slightly compromised her oesophagus when she eats, causing the wind and the burping. To be honest, my girl was more of a tomboy as she loves splashing in puddles, blowing bubbles by submerging her nose in mud and rolling in stinky things. She's never been ladylike, and this really is just another enhancement to this persona! There is no mistaking it now...

ONE PAW AT A TIME

Monday 20th January

It's been a few days, and Reba has tried using her front paw better. Still knuckled mostly but slightly less, even when she is free roaming downstairs and pottering to me. I can see her pad going down a few times which is a huge improvement.

Yesterday I decided I needed to get out, and there is a coffee truck that visits our local dog walking spot twice a week. I drove up there, with the view that if I can get parked close and see if she will walk over the stony car park to the truck, then I can sit and have a coffee, and she can meet other people and dogs as they queue for their drinks. She enjoyed it, got some fuss, and then I wanted to try her out on the path. Well, she scampered along, fell over once or twice, but was really keen to explore. We did about 20m along the heath, past some trees and she loved sniffing to catch up on all the info she has missed out on. Her legs were very uncoordinated, her back right was overcompensating for the dodgy left front and she struggled to remain straight as she moved forward, but this is all really good to see her keenness to move on.

The only downside was some quite violent leg kicks and head throwing around in her dreams later as she was lying next to me on the sofa! Happy dreaming!

I spoke to the neurologist about her dramatic head movements in her sleep. It's documented about head injuries interrupting sleep patterns, but there are fewer recorded cases of neck trauma causing the same but it does happen, and she feels that her REM sleep is disrupted by the injury.

Today, we had the mobile vet visit with her assistant, so they could give Reba her acupuncture. Reba was so excited to have new visitors, we did have a few flying nuggets leak out! We struggled to get a time in the diary this week, so the vet offered the therapy at our home. Reba struggled to stay calm, but we got through it, and she coped well. We all agreed that she was better at the practice, but the vet was really pleased to see her at home, and how she can move around. I showed her the video from yesterday's walk too, so she can have a good idea on where to focus the needles based on Reba's movement/restrictions.

Tuesday 21st January

Rough night, as she woke me about 4.30 a.m. We ended up having quite a lie-in though which was nice, but I'm still tired.

We had the groomers today, so took the buggy to push her up the hill from the car park. As she is standing really well, it was agreed that I wasn't needed in the salon to hold her. I went to my favourite café, only for it to be shutting early! Nooo! There are a few other cafés, so sat down with my book, but the flapjack was crumbly and had coconut in it, so not very enjoyable. Went back up the hill, in time for the groomer to need my help as Reba was literally kicking off about her nail trim. She was fine for the sharp scissors trimming between her toes and pads but was refusing the nails. Even with me holding her, she was twisting, getting out of the supports (she can only have one on her belly and under her waist, never on her neck) and fighting. It was a challenge with two of us so I will need to work out why she is really not liking it anymore. Maybe her sensitivities are changed.

As I was loading her back into her buggy, her nose appeared out the back, then her bum - she had managed to prise the zip apart! My wonderful groomer grabbed her keys and helped us back to the car park - I carried the lump whilst she steered the buggy. I wouldn't have managed without her and was so lucky we were the last client of the day.

She looks fab and smells so wonderful, and will stay like that for longer than normal as she is not out walking and rolling in stuff.

We've been practising the lie down to stand physio exercise, and she is really good at this. She does protest a bit about going into a lie down, but I put this down to more wanting the treat in my hand and frustration, as I only give her the treat once she has pushed herself up to standing.

Wednesday 22nd January

Ended up doing a bit of a walk on the heath this morning, so she can have some sniffing enrichment as well as meeting other dogs and people. Despite it being dry, it was fairly quiet up there, but she did have some hops and smelling of the greenery, we managed about 20m. All her legs are going different speeds, and her rear right is overcompensating reaching forward. I'm sure with practice and time, it will all come together a bit more as her muscle tone increases, and the neurons continue to heal. She is using her tail as a rudder, rather than being central and relaxed but she is moving, and that is great.

I'm hoping this tires her out as later on I'm out at the theatre, and it will be the first time she won't have me there. No panic, my lovely McTimoney lady offered to dog sit, as she also saw the play on another day (we both have birthdays this month). Reba was a bit unsettled, but I literally just went out with little fuss, and her sitter was armed with food, a new chew toy and the promise of lots of cuddles. She was astounded by the speed of Reba charging around the kitchen in excitement to her arrival!

I had a great time, and apparently so did Reba! She did a treatment on her, Reba loved the massage on her leg muscles, and even slept on her lap! I was really quick getting out of the car park and whizzed home as quickly as I could, but all was ok and that was a relief.

It was nice to have a break, and some time to not think about my situation or Reba's recovery, but on the flip side, I was also happy to be home with her.

Her new cavaletti poles arrived today. We have some but the lowest setting on the cone is too high, and a lovely separation anxiety colleague had the lower cones not being used and just posted them to me for free - how wonderful. We had a quick go, but will do a video to send later in the week to show how useful they are.

It will be the last night with the trazadone tonight too. After this, I will try without and still have six tablets should it not work out. I want to have a few spare, just in case, so it's not a rushed prescription. It went well, just the usual stirring early on but she slept well.

Thursday 23rd January

Another lie in. I've been so tired and even if I do go to bed early, it can sometimes be hard to sleep.

She's off to hydro today, and this time she's being tested on the water treadmill. They are concerned that it might not work due to her struggling to place her front paw. However, she needs to be tested. Oh my, she did so well!!! They had a little video of the second run. She was raising her paws a bit higher to above the water line sometimes – it was up to her elbows – and every four or five steps they had to help her place correctly and she was given breaks between runs. Each run was approximately 4 ½ mins and she excelled, doing very well considering it was her first ever time, and was even placing well. I did then realise that her lovely grooming shampoo smell will be less due to her going in the water, but it was only her lower half that got soggy!

I'm so impressed with how she is still fighting to improve, and how much she has done so. It's been a little over 12 weeks since the accident, and I never thought she would walk again, let alone go on a treadmill.

I thought she might be tired, but she had other ideas, so I did some more physio on her in the afternoon.

That evening, after one of her toilet breaks, she went for a drink so I went and sat on the sofa in the other room, with the expectation she will come out to me and then I can lift her up to sit next to me. As with all great plans, it never happened! She scampered into the living room, took one look and then launched herself up on the sofa – and made it! Now, this is amazing progress but can be very dangerous as she has not got the same strength as before, and could easily slip, stumble, fall and hurt herself. Now I'm going to have to step up another level of vigilance, harder as she bumbles around more and rests less.

Tonight will be the first non-sedation night, so wish me luck!

It started well, and she was quite relaxed as she lay on my bed whilst I read. Before, she would have been stressed, panting and panicked, hence why we upped the trazadone before. The big test will be when I put her down to her bed. I might read for longer to give her more time to settle.

Friday 24th January

Quite a good night! I woke about 2.30 a.m., heard some strange noises but there is a storm tonight and the winds were making a lot of noise, with the bins outside being blown over. Reba woke at a similar time, started getting out of bed and I encouraged her back, but then it took me an hour or more to get back to sleep. She had no problem, thankfully. When I woke, she was awake – very new thing as before, every morning I've had to wake her as she is still under the effects of the sedation, making her lethargic. And not only was she awake but she came over and was rubbing against my legs as I sat on the side of the bed, a bit like a cat wanting the contact and a stroke/bottom scratch. She used to do this lots before, and this is the first time she's done this since the accident. I am so pleased.

The storm has blown past here, so it's a lovely morning and I'm going out to walk on the heath with her.

She has surpassed my expectations by charging along without stopping for over 10 minutes, and was determined to carry on. We ended up doing about 20 mins, with stops, on a little loop. The ground is uneven sand, tree roots and some dips in the sand and she managed to navigate these really well, even splashing in a puddle. I used the 3m line for the first time to give her more freedom, as she is more stable. She only fell over once but when she did stop to sniff, she managed to manoeuvre herself quite well too.

This walk was probably pushing my luck in terms of distance and time, but we have not been told we can't nor any restrictions (unlike other surgeries on joints), and I was guided by Reba. It's also great enrichment as she got to meet two other dogs as well briefly, and catch up on all the latest news left behind by others.

She was still sprightly this afternoon, so I decided to video her going over the poles. It's just one, and really low, and I lured her with food to make her go super slow. The point is for her to think about all her legs in turn and where they are going, without worrying about clearing the pole if needed. What I did notice is that once the front legs are over, she is reluctant to then lead with her left rear leg, and instead adjusts to step over with her right hind leg first each time. Her left hind stretches back to the furthest point and she rarely brings it forward until it really can't stretch anymore, but by this point she has hopped to ensure the right leg steps over before it.

Showed a video from our walk today to a behaviourist friend, and she was so amazed at the progress in such a short time. Her voice note made me cry, the words were so kind. I still get emotional at times.

Saturday 25th January

Dilemma time. We didn't give the trazadone last night, and now I'm wondering whether to go back to it or not. On one hand, it is a sedation and helps her sleep, and the reason we went back to this was the fact she was getting really distressed at night. She isn't so worried now. However, last night, she got up about five times! Each time, she was out of the bed and mostly woke me as she bumped against my bed. She wasn't upset or anxious and soon went back into bed to sleep. She had a late night wee, so it wasn't that either. All these interruptions didn't help me as I also then woke up a few extra times in the night too. She's already been on this sedation for three months, and she can't stay on them. Might be brave and see what she is like for the next few nights without, and if I can get to have a night's sleep again.

It was sunny this morning, so we went out to the heath. I had not planned to do two consecutive days walking, as I certainly don't want to overdo it. Her muscle strength and stamina are low (as are mine!!) but she needs to ease into it carefully. The forecast for the next five to seven days is wet and horrible, and this is why we took the opportunity to go out. I ensured it was a shorter circle route than yesterday, and good fortune meant that we bumped into one of her best pals, Robin! His dad was so shocked to see us too. Reba fell over in excitement! As she was on a lead, they couldn't charge around but I feel it was really nice for Reba to see one of her friends. She is enjoying the walk, as there are lots of smells for her. Her default is run (in a weird, uncoordinated way) and if I hold the lead close, she can do a little bit of very slow walking as well, but she is not there with her 'trot'. Like puppies, they are all or nothing and only develop the trot as their default preference pace as they mature. Whether this is something that comes back to Reba in time is yet to be determined, so for now it's full charge or stop!

I decided not to give her the trazadone tonight, let's see if it makes any difference after a few days. Not helped by the fact that it was after I put the light out that I forgot the gabapentin tablets! Rushed downstairs, late meds but had no detrimental effect thankfully. She did a stir of padding around in a circle in the early hours but settled for the rest of the night.

Sunday 26th January

A break between the showers this morning, so took her for a little walk on the heath again, and off lead. We were on the quiet side, and she felt very comfortable to scamper around, sniffing and running, and there were no other dogs to watch out for.

The rest of the day was doing some physio, and relaxing. Not that she relaxes much, as now she can, she prefers to potter.

Tonight, she woke me up about 3 a.m., out of bed but then when I told her to go back in, she was licking the mattress. It was the first time I took the pee pad away, as she had been dry for a few weeks now.... Note: the use of 'HAD'! She had wet the bed, her special bed that she has kept nice all her life. Despite a late evening toilet, and another wee before bed, she managed to do this. Gutted, and not happy that at 3 a.m. I was finding other bedding, spraying the soiled one with loads of enzymatic cleaner and leaving in the bathtub. She slept well after, cheeky minx.

Monday 27th January

Reba had to come with me this morning out and about. Firstly, was a little run on the heath to give her a toilet break, and next she stayed in the boot of my car whilst I went food shopping. The cheaper supermarkets don't do delivery, and normally she would have stayed at home, but I've not done any training on her separation anxiety recently and at least the weather is fine for her hiding in the boot area, not getting hot. It is a risk, and a risk of theft, but I don't have many options right now.

In the afternoon, we had her next acupuncture. Her feelings are definitely returning as she sensed the needles in her paw area – a good thing if not annoying for the vet! The squeezy cheese was needed and this kept her settled whilst the needles did their trick. She was also much better in that environment, less excited, calmer and co-operative.

Apart from nighttime, she is also in the garden off lead, and sometimes with me just hanging out by the back door. Although she often prefers it if I do go out with her (not nice in this wet weather!), her confidence is building slowly.

She was on my bed as usual whilst I read for a bit, and as soon as I had got under the duvet, she started her padding around in a circle. With her knuckled front paw, she is like a three-legged table, and being on a mattress and duvet, she ended up spinning around, losing her balance and somersaulted! Literally went upside down! My heart was in my mouth, but she landed on the bed, phew. It was very funny, but she settled very quickly and stayed curled up until I carried her to her bed later.

Tuesday 28th January

She is nil by mouth this morning, as we are due to see the surgeon before lunchtime, and a possible sedation/CT scan. She is not happy! I melted a bone broth so she could have that as a little drink, but she was very confused why she had not had breakfast.

We turned up early and for the first time, she walked in, instead of me carrying her. All the receptionists were so shocked, and the surgeon was by the front desk and saw her too. He then told us there is no need for a scan. Her responses on her front and rear left paws are slow to right themselves, we have a lot of healing still to do, but the prognosis is really good. We have to continue the hydro treadmill, and he was so appreciative of all my commitment and efforts for her recovery.

We had to walk on the surgery's drive whilst he videoed her, and we can hear her scuffing her nails as she walks, so I need to ensure that nothing cuts her or they wear down, so most walking must be on grass (or the heathland), so soft surfaces only. We can then build up her muscle memory, the tone in her muscles and her mobility. He said that there are still months to go in her rehab. It will take time, but she is on track, making progress and will continue to do so.

He then wanted a picture of just him and Reba, he is quite besotted with her! He argued with his assistant as to who was going to give her the gravy bones! Once he had a cuddle, she then had her chance, and Reba was very grateful for some food!

He was so appreciative of our work, as their job might be the most dramatic with surgery, but they are there to stabilise the skeleton, however this is only part of it. The biggest part is for each owner to do the work, dedicate time and patience, and meet your dog's changing needs, as without this, they won't heal. Both parts are important, but the biggest chunk by far is the rehab after the surgery. Not everyone can take time off work (financially, I can't really but I chose to adjust my priorities so that my dog came off the 'put to sleep' list through lack of mobility). The surgeon put his hands together and gave me a huge bow out of respect for what I have done to help my dog so far. Deep down, they want this as otherwise there is less point putting your dog through risky surgery, even in our emergency situation. He then gave me a hug!

Came home and put some of her breakfast biscuits on a snuffle mat. I didn't have anything to raise it up, and once she was done, she did gag a few times so I need to get something the right height and size but also not one with solid sides so she can put her paws under. I have a storage drawer that I used before, but it keeps her toes back as there are no gaps on the sides. Might need to look around charity furniture shops soon, once Reba can be left at home, so her feeders can be raised up and take the pressure off her throat.

We did a few of her physio exercises too after lunch, and now she is quite happy resting.

Wednesday 29th January

She had a fairly quiet night – she woke up early hours and did a quick bark but soon resettled.

Early (for us!!!) start as we have the electrician here first thing to put up a wired outside light. It's on a switch so stays on and lights up as far as THAT tree! Now I won't need to go out with my headtorch on to supervise Reba in the dark.

Reba was a bit excited, so we hunkered down in the front room till he finished. As it was finally dry out, we went up to the heath for a lovely walk. Well, she runs, and I try and keep up. We were out for about 45 mins, but we stopped often to chat, so the actual walking time was only half that. It's been so long since we have walked there, a huge swathe of trees have gone alongside the main path as a 'fire break' despite the path being very wide – it's commonly known as the gallops, as horses often are seen charging up there. This happened when we were close, so I held Reba, as the last thing we needed was for her to turn, fall over, and roll down the slope in front of the three riders!

This afternoon, she was very relaxed. Since she had become more mobile, she doesn't lie down very often so this was nice to see her settle and snooze during the day.

This evening, we tried the new garden light for the first time – brilliant!

Thursday 30th January

So tired! She took hours to settle properly last night, turning around in bed till about 1 a.m., then again at 4 a.m. and again at 7 a.m.!

Now I'm letting Reba out to toilet on her own. I have to help her over the threshold step and may even have to stand outside on the patio, but she is now confident enough, and just about stable enough to manage on her own and not fall over when squatting. We are doing our physio exercises in bits during the day too, so that is keeping us busy.

I had heard of awful traffic due to some roadworks, so set off really early, only to find they had been lifted! We headed over to one of the heaths so she could have a toilet break. She really enjoyed the new smells, but I didn't want to stay too long and be late for our hydro appointment. Reba stood there watching me, quite upset and confused, when I was calling her back towards the car. I will have to visit again soon.

We ended up arriving at hydro about 15 mins early - must be one of those days today!

As we sat there, a lady in scrubs was getting a coffee from the machine next to us and she came over, asking to stroke Reba. She said that she recognised her and asked her name. Immediately after I told her, she lit up and was so excited! She told me that everyone knew Reba in the kennels area (where she worked) as not only is she an unusual cross, but her accident was very unique, and she was so lovely that during her stay, everyone was giving her lots of hugs, and even fought over who's turn it was next! This was so heartwarming to hear as, although they tell us things at the time, you never really know what happens behind closed doors, so to hear that they all loved Reba was emotional. I told her that she must have been the reason why Reba came home such a diva after being so spoilt!! A colleague of hers had joined us and was giving Reba lots of attention and agreeing with her – it was like Reba's groupies, and she was a star. Reba showed off her standing and walking too, as today I didn't carry her, but walked her in. They were amazed at her progress in this short period of time and praised me in all my efforts to get her to this point.

Her water treadmill session went well. They showed me a video, and her front paws were placing well on the slow walking, so they worked on her hind legs. She needed a few prompts but then showed that she didn't need them for a few steps, but then forgot so needed prompting again. They extended the sessions by 90 seconds today and had lower water level in there. Last week it was quite high so she had natural buoyancy, but this meant she was stretching up high with her back legs, but not really working as she was letting the water take her body, so this time she had to work harder.

She came out, immediately wanted to sit on my lap and promptly started to fall asleep, so she must have expended lots of energy in her session! We carried on talking to the lady with a Weimaraner who has mid spine issues till they went into their physio, then took Reba home.

Reba was very snoozy for a change and rested on the fluffy vet bedding next to me all afternoon.

Friday 31st January
A better night's sleep last night, not perfect but an improvement from the previous night.

After breakfast, set up her cavaletti pole so she can practise stepping over it, co-ordinating her legs. The trick is to get her to go very slow and only use one leg at a time, she still readjusts her hind legs to step first with the right, but she still has to work the left one or it gets left behind.

When she runs, she leads with her right leg all the time too, that is her strongest one and the one that healed first, and fastest.

I needed to let a friend's dog out for a midday break. They are only a short way down the road in the village, and last time I kept Reba in the car where she is happy to settle. Today, I wanted to try her home alone. I closed the kitchen door, our old routine but I've not done this since before the accident so was unsure how it would go. The reason is that I have the camera showing there – if I let her into the hallway, I won't be able to monitor her, and she will see me putting on shoes and going out the door which is more unsettling. Anyway, arrived after a two-minute drive to the house, opened the back door for the dog to toilet, and logged into the camera. Reba was standing near the kitchen door, not looking happy but not showing anxiety signs. I figured that if she stayed like this, I could spend a few more minutes with my friend's dog - so we had a cuddle on the sofa for a little bit before I packed up and went home. Reba heard me come home but was still standing just behind the door as I entered the kitchen.

I do need to start doing the home alone training again, and this occasion was a needs must scenario, but Reba coped ok. Not great, but no distress. Being a dog separation anxiety specialist, I already know the best way to approach this and build her up slowly. I'm hoping that she is now feeling much better compared to before, and she remembers about feeling safe when home alone, it will just be a slow re-introduction to this to help her. Then I might be able to go to the supermarket soon, without having her hiding in the boot – I do worry about her safety, from the temperature to dog theft but I don't have the choice right now.

Saturday 1st February

I can't believe it's now 14 weeks since her accident and operation and look where we are. I have been taking her for 15-20 min walks off lead on the heath now when the weather is dry and today was one of those days. She sniffed a few dogs – I did ask their owners to ensure their dogs didn't start nudging her for play as I'm worried she will fall over, and the last thing she needs is an overactive boisterous labrador! The interaction is good for her, however she runs with a slight bend

118

to the right and always leads with the right paw. Her only pace is a run which is exhausting to keep up with! But she stops often, and this is why we keep the walks short, so that she can slowly build up her stamina and muscle tone. I am conscious of her only doing as she is now, overreaching with one hind leg, dragging the other as the mobility style, so I need to ensure we do more physio than walks right now, to even her up.

She has been waking once or twice in the night, often before 3 a.m. but thankfully she then resettles and sleeps through, so not too bad. I'm still waiting for the cushion insert to arrive so she can go back to her normal bed which has a softer covering so quieter when she moves around in the night, but she still has the pee pad on just in case.

Sunday 2nd February

I've not even put her harness on today – she's nude!!! We are having our neighbour's dog pop over later as they are going out for a few hours, so instead of a walk, he's coming here. He will be so excited as he LOVES Reba and has been sniffing the fence lots to see if she is in our garden!

I was at the table, enjoying a cuppa when she scrambled around to the back door, so I opened it to let her out – and wish I hadn't! She raced down the lawn, barely missing THAT tree, and flipped on her side, rolling over a full circle before coming to a rest... in the spot too where she pooed that morning! My heart was in my mouth as she whizzed past the tree by inches, if that. I'm not sure if my body can cope with such drama. The tree is just surrounded by grass, as a few years ago I reduced the borders as they were too much for me to cope with. Now, maybe I need to plant a bit around that tree as more of a barrier and cushion. Might have to think about what I can do, or what to put there. I don't need this stress!!!

Well, Bertie came over for an hour, he was very happy to see her, sniffing her, then off exploring in our garden. Reba, to be fair, was at best nonchalant and really didn't bother! I was expecting some play, or some exploring together, but she didn't even go outside with him. Never mind. Bertie spent half the time snoozing at my feet, Reba snoozing on the vet bedding near me.

We did some physio later and then chilled. She woke me up unsettled at 4 a.m. and I had to get up to put her back into her bed but then she slept better after that.

Monday 3rd February

Earlier start as we have a morning acupuncture appointment. Apparently, the surgeon had written an email to the vets, saying they were very happy with Reba's progress. They agreed that she would not be at the stage she is now if it hadn't been for all our hard work. As we waited in reception, Reba was shaking a bit and singing, but once we got in, she stood on the table and was so relaxed whilst they put the needles in and then waited for the time to elapse before they were removed again. The reflexes on her skin were good, and she had them down her rear left hind for the first time. We are now at a two-week interval before the next appointment.

ONE PAW AT A TIME

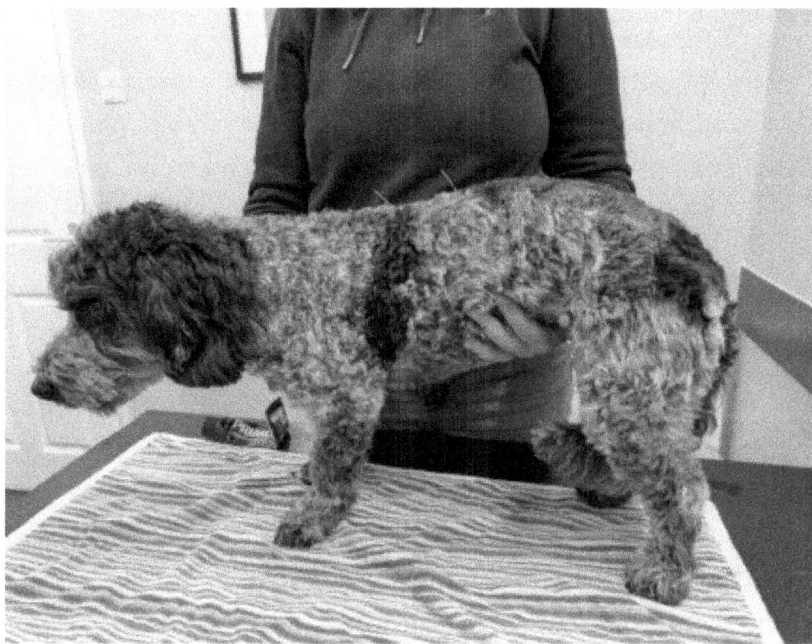

Tuesday 4th February

We had a rough night. About 2.30 a.m., she was scrabbling around, then I heard her on the bedroom floor. When I woke and told her to go back to bed, she stood there leaning over it and licking it – a sign I've learnt from recently that this means she has wet the bed. On went the light, and thankfully I've been keeping the pee mat on her bed, so this immediately got sprayed, and into the washing machine ready to be switched on first thing after we get up. I put the spare clean mat down on her mattress, plonked her in her bed (I was tired!!) and settled back down to sleep. She woke me a further two times, but not for a wet bed. She had a long wee before bed, but had refused to go out mid-evening, so maybe that is why her bladder filled again, who knows, but tonight I will try and enforce more evening toileting. Just as I think we have cracked it, she does this again. We haven't had any little brown nuggets, so she is managing to hold them in much better now and will only poo outside after breakfast, and again at lunchtime, which was very much her old routine. And the wee is 98% better too, with her holding it and indicating when she wants to go, and managing to wait until she is outside on the grass too, but there is still a risk of nighttime accidents, which is a pain as once this stops – if it ever will – then I can remove the pee pads from her bed, and her moving around will be much quieter and less likely to wake me each time.

Lots of admin today, so we've had a play in the garden, and lots of physio exercises indoors too.

I'm not feeling as energetic today, as I'm now starting to stress more about finances as the self-employment is not good and not getting any success in even getting interviews for remote jobs. I'm spending over £640 a month on her treatments now, which is pretty scary sums. This is, of course, over and above her vet bills and prescription costs. Being winter, the heating is on more too.

Wednesday 5th February

She woke me about six times last night, between 2 a.m. and 7 a.m. The first was when she was out of the bed, the rest with her just resettling. Your brain adjusts to noises and how to respond... when I was an on-call firefighter, I could sleep through storms, but I was up and already getting dressed at the sound of the first beep from the bleeper. This is the same, I've self-conditioned myself to respond to her moving, and this was from the very first night she came home after the accident. Now it's coming to haunt me as the noise from her temporary bed, and the pee pad, make her moving around louder as well, but I'm automatically waking up to check up on her.

We went to see Nana this morning. One big difference was her moving around. Last time, she was only lying on the pee pad in the kitchen, as she was less mobile (sometimes trying only one or two steps) but also still fairly incontinent, and Mum's house is carpeted, except for the kitchen. Today, Reba was moving quite well on the vinyl floor as it had a bit of texture on it, and we were both confident enough to let her potter around on the carpets. She was even able to mooch outside on her own too, but we kept close watch on her through the window. When we moved into the sitting room, Reba was sizing up about jumping up on the sofa, but I managed to grab her and pick her up. She snoozed on my lap until we had to go.

After a quick lunch at home, we went for a potter on the heath and met one of my friends up there – she had not heard about the accident as we normally just chat when we bump into each other up there (I have several 'friends' that I only meet that way), but this one is a great artist and did a fantastic pencil portrait of Reba.

Quite a busy day of enrichment for Reba today, so will rest her on the physio a bit and pick up all the exercises again tomorrow, as she is shattered from all the exertion. She doesn't rest much during the day now, so all this exploring and visiting will give her a chance to rest and recover.

Thursday 6th February

Apart from a little bark and stirring in the early hours, Reba slept most of the night, which was a relief - I could get some sleep too.

She was getting fidgety this morning, so I took her for a little potter around the heath. I had to body block a young labrador twice, but thankfully the owners hung back and gave us space to move on up the path – there are three parallel paths all starting and ending the same point, so of course they followed me on the one I was on. Quite often passers-by comment that she is lame, and look at me badly, but once I say that she is actually recovering from a broken neck, their attitude flips quickly to tell me how well she is doing. It's easy to be judgemental without knowing the full story, and it's hard not to be when we see a wobbly dog struggling to follow their owner on a walk. You have to think whether the dog is really up for it, but in our case, it's part of her healing, a very different situation.

She had her third water treadmill session at lunchtime. They lowered the water again, and extended the times – she did an eight-minute walk today! They found that she responded better to them 'tickling' her feet rather than placing them for her, and she walked lovely. She was quite curved around when I took her back to the car, but she must be really tired after the activity today.

Friday 7th February

Had a really good night's sleep last night. I was only woken up by Reba stirring and out of her bed, and once I got up, I saw that there was a brown nugget by her bed, and one in it. This is a much easier accident to clean up.

After breakfast, she became playful – a lovely change. She was grabbing a toy, letting me hold it for a few seconds (she never plays tug) and then dropped it so I could throw it. Of course I didn't launch it far, but if you just watched her, you would never know that it only went a few feet, not the length of the room which is what she ran across!

Our lovely McTimoney lady came over, and Reba was still energetic. She lay on her bed chewing a toy whilst I was making our guest a cuppa, and chatting about her progress on the other therapies when Reba suddenly stopped chewing and looked around at her bottom – apparently, she had just farted and surprised herself!

She soon settled into the treatment, standing lovely and square for the first part of checking her spine alignment – she has only ever been lying down for this. Then she lay down for the start of the massage. It's easy for the therapist to treat the right side, and her muscles were becoming much more formed on that side, but to get to the left, Reba is not happy to lie down that way so we ended up with Reba snuggled on my lap whilst I was on the floor, and she could then lay on her least preferred side for the massage on her weaker left.

Reba was enjoying it so much, she was almost purring! She was so relaxed, and quite sleepy after too - well, until the doorbell went.

It's horrible weather outside today, so we will do our indoor exercises and go back out on a walk tomorrow when it's due to be drier.

Saturday 8th February

Rainy day today, and Reba was in a playful mood this morning. Apart from a big resettling about 1 a.m., she'd slept through the night.

Still decided to go out for a short walk. The road to the heath was closed with roadworks so I carried on to the hill, as there is a buggy/ stony path that does a short loop, the rest is really muddy and slippery so I thought great, we can avoid the worst of the mess. Oh no, we didn't! The path descended into mud at the far end, really squelchy, and puddly. And of course, she fell over in it. Covered on one side. And then it really started to rain from the slight drizzle when we started. We only did 15 mins, but it looked like we had been out much longer.

I've not tried bathing Reba myself yet, as I used to use a suction noose to hold her into the bathtub, but of course she can't have anything around her neck now, and not quite worked out what we can do. Might just let her dry off, brush off the rest and plan a bath for another day soon.

I was enjoying my cuppa at the dining table, and realised Reba had got up, no big deal. I thought she might have gone to the back door but when I moved, she wasn't in the kitchen, nor the living room – found her at the base of the stairs and as I approached, she looked like she was sizing up going up the first step. Managed to distract her and call her away as she can barely manage the one on the patio, let alone a whole flight. She was trying to go back to bed! It's only early afternoon, far too early for that, although tempting.

That night, I noticed that her front left nails were splitting where she is scuffing them. I need to keep an eye on this as it could damage to the quick – the nerve and blood supply. There are things like little tubes – toe protectors on the claws but not sure how she will take to them. I try and keep her to soft surfaces, so may have to look for some temporary covering on the patio between the door and the lawn too. I think today's unexpected walk did more damage.

Sunday 9th February

About 2 a.m., she woke me and kept me awake for about five minutes as she was struggling to settle and get comfortable. We switched back the beds for her as the foam insert arrived. Finally, she went back to sleep and allowed both of us to get some good rest.

Since the accident, I've had to try and grab a shower and hair wash when she was still in bed in the mornings, as the sedation was still making her sleepy. If I had tried to go to the bathroom when she was awake, she would cry and whine, very distressed. Now she is more mobile, she is feeling much better in herself to allow me to go the bathroom (I only have the one upstairs) and leave her downstairs. Lately, there has been no anxiety, so I decided to mix it up this morning. I actually went downstairs in my dressing gown, carrying her with me. We had our breakfast, then I left her down there whilst I had a non-rushed shower by myself. Bliss! Even time to dry my hair afterwards. There was no separation distress at all, no barking, no crying, nothing. Brilliant! I will add that also before, I had to rush to get her downstairs and take her outside, and hold her whilst she toileted, so another reason to rush to get dressed before she woke up. Nowadays, she can hold it by choice till after her breakfast, and then go out on her own. Neighbours won't see me in my PJs!

This is really getting back to our old routine.

We went up to the heath for a walk, and once we were past the car park and gate, I put her down and we headed in. She suddenly sprinted along the path – I was so shocked at the speed, but also the fact she was totally ignoring me. I guessed that she must have smelt a friend up ahead, as this is the only time she does this (unless there is a picnic up ahead, but it's too cold for that!). She stopped once at one of my calls, looked at me, ignored me and ran ahead. Over the brow of the small hill, I could see a group of people ahead with two smallish dogs, likely cockerpoo size. Anyway, on she charged and howled with excitement, and I could see who it was – her old friend Roo and his humans. Reba was beside herself, so happy. Roo was leaping up at me for attention, and his humans were so overjoyed to see Reba doing happy zoomies. They have been following her progress on my social media, and I think they were impressed to see just how she was in real life.

All this exertion meant she got tired sooner, so we only did a short loop so she could go home and rest.

Monday 10th February

She woke me about six times last night, at one point every hour. It's the noise of her trying to get comfortable, and can go on for minutes at a time.

Saw the forecast, so after breakfast I took her for a walk on the heath. She is still bunny hopping her rear legs and her left hip is held lower than the right side, so quite lopsided.

One thing I have noticed is that she is better going up the step on the patio. Before, she would stop and think, then place her front right up, then after a minute, place the other front leg up, then wait a minute or two, and then bunny hop her back legs onto the step. I want to encourage her to do this herself, not lift her every time, so that she starts to use her brain for leg placement. Once or twice, she has fallen, but over the last week, she is improving. She still places the front right up, but within 30 seconds, she then is fairly fluid in moving all three other legs up at the same time (in slow motion it will show that there are separate movements). And she's not stumbling so much immediately afterwards. As soon as she in on the grass, she can run, although her hips wobble from side to side and push her off balance, but mostly she can right herself even if she cannot manage a straight line yet.

This may not seem like much for most owners, but for us, now, this is a huge improvement.

Tuesday 11th February

Went up to the heath car park for a walk in the late morning, and as I arrived, a previous client with his spaniel were just finishing their walk, and we often bump into each other – well, when we were walking regularly – so we had a little chat. As I did, another past client and now friend had arrived with her two small terriers, so we agreed to walk together. I explained that I couldn't go far but she didn't mind. We went slow, and actually Reba was going slower too, which was good for her to think about a different speed to running (lopsidedly). Part way around, I came across yet another past client/friend and Reba was very excited to see little Louis! She darted over, fell over, and then Louis took it up on himself to chase off another approaching dog! It was very exciting for Reba to bump into several of her small dog friends, and I had a lovely chat with the terrier mum too.

We did stop a few times, so it was not all go, but we ended up taking an hour on the shorter loop! We plan to co-ordinate properly again soon, as the dogs were lovely together and really enjoyed themselves.

All this effort meant that I had a very sleepy dog this afternoon. She also slept better at night too, only once waking me up with her shuffling around.

Wednesday 12th February

I had a meeting this morning with a local business owner that I do occasional work for, and had to leave Reba at home. I was not sure how she would cope as we have not practiced being home alone. It was in the village, so I was not far, but my new mobile provider was rubbish and had no reception to check the pet camera. Thankfully, the meeting place had guest WIFI and Reba looked fine, standing by the door to begin with, but then she lay down near the door. No anxiety, but I didn't want to push my luck.

Once I got home, I bundled her into the car for a walk, then she stayed in the boot whilst I did a sneaky supermarket run. On the way back I had to pop back into their office, but they love Reba and were super impressed with her mobility so far.

Not having the pet camera is a real problem. My last mobile provider was fine, but this one has been a nightmare with false promises, no support, and now locked in for 24 months – the cost to leave is extortionate and I certainly don't have the budget. So angry, as it's not only my work phone, but I absolutely need to have the camera to check on Reba so that I can build up her separation anxiety tolerance again. I need to be able to watch her body language, the basics of the training so I'm not away longer than she can cope with and get distressed.

Thursday 13th February

We had our catch up with the physio today. Reba managed to solicit attention in the waiting room, and then she decided to be on my lap, so I ended up carrying her in. Quickly back on the floor, she was snuffling around really well. Most of the room has this non-slip matting on it, so very safe for all wobbly dogs. The physio was really impressed, as she had been worried that the last exercises may have been too much. In fact, we have a list of a lot more advanced pole work. She even had scrunchies on her ankles, as this small bit of pressure can help lift her legs more. Reba looked so cute!! Her paw sensitivity is much improved, as the physio found out when Reba squealed at her and ran to me!

They soon became friends again when the gravy bones appeared. It was a really positive session, and the physio could see just how hard we have worked. Feeling very happy.

Reba was shattered afterwards, as all that thinking is tiring.

Friday 14th February

Valentine's Day! It's just us so we will have extra sofa cuddles tonight.

This morning, she had her McTimoney treatment. She was super excited when our lady arrived and went charging down the garden – which also showed what her movements are like now. There was just a bit of treatment needed on her hips, as Reba is using her right side to motor along and not using her left as much. When it came to the massage, she was dozing off and loving it. So much so, when the massage around her right chest/leg area was ending, she was batting the therapist gently with her paw to get her to continue! There were sighs of contentment throughout. This part of her treatment is essential to keep the stronger side more relaxed and healthier, whilst the left side catches up.

I was told to not take her out today, so we had a chill out day instead.

Saturday 15th February

She woke me a few times last night, almost like sleepwalking. I would look over and she is standing on the rug, totally still. This happened a few times - once I had to gently touch her but otherwise, she responded to me telling her to go back to bed. Before 8 a.m. (I know you early risers are scoffing at me, but I haven't had a good night's sleep!), she suddenly was standing up, barking. I was very thankful that I have the stairgate at the top of the stairs, but she did resettle. Later I found out it was a very early parcel delivery!

A little walk on the heath, and she is much more stable, and falling over less. She is noticeably correcting herself better but still looking quite drunk. We ended up stopping a few times. She managed to get lots of attention and a few gravy bones (from someone I know), but I am also staying very close, ready to pick her up or body block for the younger, larger dogs that come over. I'm still sensitive to a dog surprising her so she flips her head round fast, or if they try and play and possibly knock her over. Not knowing their play styles, or anything about them, I would rather be cautious. She can happily go and run with her friends, as I trust them and they are also very careful with her, always have been with each other.

The promised sunshine never materialised, instead it started to rain, and it was freezing cold, so we didn't hang around too much before going home.

Sunday 16th February

It's going to be tough for the next 10 days to do her physio, as we have one of her little best friends over to stay. He's really good and gentle, but not sure how I can cover the floor with all her poles and get her to work whilst he is watching or possibly join in, as if there are treats in my hand, he will be doing the work as well! Wish me luck! It will be good for Reba socially and mentally having him here, and I will have to take them for walks but thankfully his owner is very understanding that it may not be the level of walk he normally does, or the duration and she is totally accepting of this.

We did a little walk in the morning. The sun was out but chilly. Reba fell over a few times when she went off the path under the pine trees but overall, she is much more stable. A quick coffee and chat at the end – we bumped into some training clients of mine and their dog, and was lovely to see them again.

Home in time for Byron, and Reba was so excited to see him! His mum was impressed with how much she has improved since she last saw her. Both dogs were noisy and playful, so we sprinkled some frozen peas on the lawn for them to forage whilst his mum snuck out, so that he didn't get too upset. Now they are chilled out on the beds/flooring behind me.

Monday 17th February

Woken up by Reba. I could hear her padding about and looked around, and there she was, standing by my bed, looking up at me. Grabbed her and carried her down the stairs – she was excited, and I thought it was because Byron was at the bottom. Found out later it was because she needed a poo, as one dropped onto the stairs!

She was happy to see him, so I put her down, and they both rushed to the back door where she barged past him and both ran out, up the little step and down the garden, and it was as if she had no mobility issues at all. And yes, she needed the toilet!

When done and breakfast was eaten, she was trying to instigate play with him. He was not responding this morning to her advances, and just sat there, even when she wobbled into him. So proud of her for trying.

It makes me quite upset to see the difference between these times, and when she is more tired, like last night when she struggled to get to the lawn, her back legs were crossing over, and she was wobbling a lot. There was more scuffing of her nails too as she tried but failed to walk to the lawn area. The new strip of artificial grass is out for delivery, and I plan to have this going from the step up to the patio right up to the lawn so she can go along without dragging or damaging her nails.

We had a great little walk on the heath before lunch, as she has her acupuncture this afternoon. I left Byron in the car outside the vets – I had a space right outside the door, and the vet is tucked away in a village so fairly secure, but otherwise he would be too much of a distraction. Reba coped brilliantly, standing there during the treatment. She can now feel some of the needles in her lower front leg, as it is more sensitive there now – a good thing that her feeling is really coming back down that leg. It's a good chance to chat to the vet, too, about her progress whilst we wait for the magic to happen.

It was just a relaxed evening with all of us cuddling on the sofa tonight, very enjoyable.

Tuesday 18th February

I woke before her today and had to get her up. She does wait for me to pick her up to carry her down the stairs. Byron was excited to see her, however once again, after breakfast, Reba was trying to incite some play, but Byron took himself back to bed and fell asleep. Poor Reba, she's finally mobile enough to want to play but her normally reliable friend is having none of it! He's only five months older than her but it seems he's five years older, a real old man... in his mind.

They were both mithering me to go out, so we did, however it may look sunny but its FREEZING! We did a different short loop, maybe a few 100m longer, and I could tell when Reba was tiring as she slowed down, then stopped for me to carry her.

They relaxed in the afternoon whilst I had some work calls. It's harder to do physio with Reba with her pal here. As soon as I get the treats out, he is all over me, and won't stand aside, and is knocking over the poles more than Reba does. May have to just rely on the walks for now and then work on the exercises once he is gone and we have the space, and less distractions for her. I can still do some of the earlier work such as stimulating her paws, and I am working on getting her desensitised to the nail clippers again so not all lost.

We have some therapies this week too, so Byron can stay in the car whilst Reba has her workouts.

Wednesday 19th February

Reba was quite fidgety last night, so I woke a few times in the night. She's bright as a button this morning - me, not so.

Spent the morning working and doing admin, and thankfully she was quite settled. We ended up doing a longer walk today at lunchtime. The sun was out, she was coping well and so I went just a bit further. She did start to struggle towards the end so carried her the last section towards the car. What I did notice is that when she slowed down, and did walk, she managed about four or five steps on her front left with the paw in the correct position before she started knuckling again. This is really good progress, as before, anything other than a run, she was over on that leg. If she stops to sniff, she is right down over her wrist which is not great, but each extra step with her paw corrected is brilliant.

I stopped off at the vets on the way back, to hand over a big box of chocolates. They have been brilliant, from that night right through to all the calls about her meds after she came home, to the great acupuncture and care they have shown on each visit. I'm sure they will be very much appreciated, I certainly appreciate them as they are independent and so the care is brilliant. I nearly cried when I told them why I had bought them a treat, as without them, things could have been so different.

Tonight, I made sure that she had both a mid-evening and a late evening wee, as I wanted to risk not having the pee pad on her mattress and see if removing that means she can shuffle around in bed and not wake me up.

Thursday 20th February

Success – an undisturbed night! It helped that we did a much longer walk in the day, so she was tired. But no accidents in her bed, phew!

We did a much shorter walk this morning, as not only is it raining but she also has hydrotherapy today and I didn't want to tire her out too much.

Her therapy session went very well. She was a bit more vocal today and this is common in dogs that now realise they are much better and protest a bit more with the assistance. On the treadmill, the water is only halfway up her legs, and her front paw hardly knuckled at all. However, the rear left is now her weakest and needs prompting often, and she loses her balance more easily too. We need to trigger the nerves more in her foot, as once this paw gets better, she will balance more on my flooring too. And she may stop bunny hopping and actually running and trotting more in sync too. They noticed that she has a lot more muscle tone coming back to the left side, which is fantastic, and shows her strength is increasing.

Byron was most put out as Reba went straight to his bed after we came home from hydro and fell asleep there! Only when he barked at a phantom person at the door, which got her up, did he managed to sneak back in.

Friday 21st February

Awful night last night. Just as I put her to bed and switched the light off, she got up and stood on the rug by my bed. She's almost in a trance and can't hear me, so I have to touch her to get a response, almost like she is sleepwalking. She has done this a few times recently and last night it was five times - once I had to lift her back into bed. Finally, she slept and stayed in bed, and as she only had one wee before bed, I did put the pee mat back over her mattress.

Nice walk today. Reba met a few known friends on the heath, and one had not seen her since she was in the buggy, so almost didn't recognise her running to her.

Saturday 22nd February

Back to a good night's sleep again, she only stood up in a daze once, a short while after I switched the light out but then slept through.

I was really impressed with her this morning as she stepped out, up onto the patio, and stopped. Normally this is when her front paw is knuckled over onto her wrist, but she instantly lifted her paw a bit, and then it was still tipped over at the toes, so she lifted her leg again and now the paw flipped over and she was standing perfectly. It was all in just a few seconds, but she could obviously feel and sense it and corrected herself TWICE! Just a shame I couldn't capture this on camera, it was lucky I was watching her.

We joined my friend on a walk today and travelled to another walking spot, which is mostly sand. We stayed on the lower part and avoided the mud where they have been doing forestry work, and the large hill. It was still a reasonable walk and a bit longer than ideal, and Reba was so wobbly at the end that I had to carry her the last 100 metres. She slows, then she just stops and that is when she really has had enough. She did well though, and managed to lower herself down to try and roll in something, so she is definitely feeling better!

Sunday 23rd February

Dull day today, so we went to the heath for a shorter walk after yesterday's exploring. I took the yellow lead slip cover, which says 'Keep Dogs Away' and although she is mostly off lead, I carried it so it could be seen, and was ready to clip it on. Good job we did. Despite the car parks being rammed full, we didn't meet too many dogs but on approaching a crossroads, two lively gundogs were flying towards us. I put the lead on Reba so I could hold her up, and body block the lively large breeds (to ensure they didn't fly into her or knock her over), however their owners saw my lead and called their (very responsive) dogs back and held onto them. They said they saw the yellow, a sign of anxious dogs. That was really lovely of them, and I said it was because she was healing and wobbly, not that she is reactive. They still held onto their dogs as they went past - very kind of them. Then from the side was a couple with two spaniels – and it turns out one of the owners was one of the vet staff at our local practice, and they recognised Reba. She was super impressed with Reba's mobility compared to previously, but she also kept her spaniels away as one of hers was nervous and she was carrying a yellow warning lead.

We snuggled up on the sofa in the afternoon to watch a movie and relax. Reba is giving more warning for toileting, although I will carry her out for certain times, just to make sure we don't have accidents in the night. Without the pee pad on her mattress, nights are much quieter now, too, as I can't hear her shuffling to a new position in the night.

Monday 24th February

Whilst her buddy is staying, in the mornings I am carrying Reba down the stairs and then placing her on the ground before opening the stair gate. Byron is super happy to see her each morning, but today he accidently knocked her over, so her legs were off the mat area and on a narrow bit of slippery floor, and against the closed living room door, so she was stuck! Had to pick her up and enable her to scamper after Byron, ready to go out into the garden.

Met a past client and her two lovely little dogs for a walk. We often see them on the heath, and have walked together before, and her girls are very considerate to Reba too. Byron met these new ladies, and Reba was instantly divorced, as he was very enamoured with the new entourage! We ended up a bit further along the heath than I would have liked, as we could see some big groups of dogs on the shorter path. It must have rained lots last night as it was so puddly, more than normal, and a bit muddy in places where I had to put the lead on Reba to stop her sliding into the mud. However, she managed to fall over and land in one of the large puddles, of course a muddy one, not a new, fresh, clean one. She was very tired at the end, and it was probably too much for her so will give her an easier few days to recover.

Byron is still here for another couple of days, and then we will have less chaos, and be able to not walk if needed and concentrate on her physio. We did bump into a lovely couple on the walk, and they commented on how well Reba was doing – they last saw her when she was in the buggy and I was pushing her around the heath, so they were so happy to see that she is mobile now.

Tuesday 25th February

I had a Zoom consult this morning, so left the door open for them so they can go out if needed. However, halfway through, there was a lot of chomping noises coming from Reba. She had chewed off one arm from her monkey toy and was busy chewing the foot. I managed to get it off her, as it still had the stuffing in, but she had eaten the fabric limb, Worryingly, it also had a small amount of stuffing in that she had gobbled too. The other limb has two large holes in, so that may need amputating with scissors before she gets it back. The monkey had done quite well, with only losing the ears and tail before. She does have a habit of chewing fabric toys, so I do need to keep a close eye on them, and this one stayed intact for some considerable time compared to others! She's never had a blockage, and this means I'm not too worried about her swallowing the body parts.

We walked on the heath, and my plan was a shorter walk after yesterday's social outing. Just before we turned back to the car park, I saw a dog walker with seven large, boisterous labrador types running down the path, which would have been a safety risk for Reba, so we ended up adding an extra 10-minute loop onto the walk. Reba really struggled for that last bit, and kept stopping, and then a slow walk. The slow walk is actually good as it means she can independently move her legs in a controlled way, instead of the energetic bunny hopping, which is not good for her spine, her stamina, and her tail as that becomes a rudder. She is very tired now and sleeping.

Wednesday 26th February

It's raining lots again today, so our morning walk is delayed until it eases up a bit, as none of us like going out in it. It did look brighter, but we left, it was still raining a bit. The heath was flooded, muddy and awful. We kept the walk short and then it was time to take Byron home. Of course, the sun came out later that day!

Reba was shattered after all the fun, as they had a lovely little play session in the morning and her mobility was fab – she was running up and down the room, even on the slippery bits and didn't fall over. Now, she can barely even hold her front legs up when squatting for a wee, looks like she is lying on her belly to toilet. She only had one evening wee, so I put the pee pad back on her bed, much to her disgust, but I just can't trust her to trash it again, nor can I afford to keep replacing it.

Thursday 27th February

No walking today, I want to give her a day off. Instead, we are doing the pole work for her physio. Even when I stop, she still is going back and forth over them without me even asking, probably to still earn a treat at the end. I am using food to make sure she slows down, as I can control her speed when it's in my hand and I can lure her slowly and she can then think about stepping over properly. It works more than it doesn't, she still sneaks in some jumps occasionally. She had the scrunchies on her feet too today, so cute!

I went to sit at my desk to do some work and after a while, looked over but she was not in the three dog beds in the room. Eventually found her just around the corner snoozing on the back door mat, she didn't to go out but no idea why she chose there. She does still surprise and puzzle me even after all our years together.

Friday 28th February

We had her regular McTimoney this morning. First off, she loves having her right front massaged, so was super happy to lie on her side, legs outstretched and batting the arm of her therapist to indicate which leg she wanted treated first. The rear right took a few goes as she got a bit more fidgety, and then she wanted to get up to the sunshine outside before the left side was started. She still struggles to lay on the floor for all of it so she lies on my lap instead. Textbook – no, unorthodox – yes, but it works for us. Reba even fell asleep on my lap with her head in my arms, whilst I sat on the floor with her.

Her other therapies concentrate on the nerve messages on the left side, however the right is very tight and overworked where she overcompensates, so this regular treatment is even more important. Without her stronger right side, she will be struggling so much more. Her spine is straighter, her muscle tone is improving too, and she was less tight than last week so all good and heading in the right direction.

We need to take a friend's dog out today, so rather than rest after the treatment, she will be going walking with us, but I did warn my friend that it will only be a very short walk.

It's the first time taking the 'mad Poppy' out with Reba, and I knew the main challenge would be having both on lead in the car park. Firstly, I need to catch Poppy as she explodes out of the car – she is a springer spaniel, old, with two fused ankles but you would never believe it! I decided to put Reba out of the car first, on the lead before letting Pops out. That worked, but then Poppy charged ahead, and Reba dragged behind, making crossing the car park very interesting for me! Once off lead, they were fine, they stayed close, Poppy doing the spaniel circles, and then she was marginally better back on lead approaching the car again. Success!

Chill out afternoon as Reba has done a lot today. And she slept all night too, wonderful.

Saturday 1st March

I can't believe that the accident seems like such a long time ago, but it's only four months. In that time, my girl has gone from near death, quadriplegic to now walking and running (ok, not perfectly but she's mobile!). Incredible. Dogs heal so much faster than humans. I would still be laid up in a hospital bed at this point.

She's going more 'off-piste', or should I say 'off-mat' indoors, and will go under the dining table, and lie down by the patio doors in the sunshine. I can hear her nails scuffing on the wood floors, and the uneven patter where her leg drags along. The therapist yesterday did notice that her hind leg doesn't drag quite as far before she corrects it, so a very small improvement.

A speedy food shop and we did a quick walk after, it's such a chilly but sunny day. The heath was really quiet – busy car park and just ramblers, no dogs. That suits us fine as I am having to quickly assess each dog we come across – size, energy levels, how they greet us, as I have to be careful on Reba's neck.

Tonight, she went crazy about 90 mins after bedtime, so had to let her out into the garden again. She only did one toilet before bed, but thankfully she settled down again soon after.

Sunday 2nd March

Reba woke me before 7 a.m., so I told her to go back to bed so I could get more sleep. I woke about 9 a.m. in a blind panic – I knew we had a morning acupuncture session booked, and was convinced it was Monday! Really was convinced we would be late...and ended up checking two different sources before I realised it was Sunday, and no appointments! This is my life now – worrying about which vet practice to go to!

Now that I can relax, we had a late breakfast, then a sunny walk on the heath. One of the first people we met had two spaniels, and one came to sniff Reba and then left her alone, and went and stood by their owner, about five ft away. The owner then got out a packet of food, and the spaniel instantly charged at Reba and went to attack her neck – Reba was on lead, waiting by me at the time and no provocation at all. This spaniel must be a resource guarder, that is my only assumption. The owner instantly called her dog and was apologetic, and Reba was just a bit stunned but unharmed. I quickly ended our conversation and moved on. We then met this older gent we see often, he has two cockerpoos, and calls Reba 'splodge' due to her markings. One of his, though, was nudging Reba's neck in an attempt to get her to play, so I had to hold it back by its harness and then we quickly parted ways. A bit of drama today.

The rest of the walk was calm. We went via the cricket pitch as we had to park on the road leading to the car park. This meant that not only did I have to carry Reba up the road at the start of the walk, but also had to carry her back. Reba insisted on going up to the coffee cart where the lovely lady came out to see her and was so impressed with how she is doing. Reba then parked herself by the trailer and refused to move for quite some time. I picked her up and she rested her head on my shoulder whilst watching the lady at work brewing coffees for the queue there. I carried her up the road to the car, and we got home safely.

Monday 3rd March

Not quite a panic this morning as I knew the date and time for our acupuncture appointment! Reba was livelier at this session, you could see her body reacting to some of the needles, as it twitches, and at one point, when the vet was checking one needle, she leapt up. I managed to hold her up, but very conscious that my hands had moved so likely to disrupt or dislodge a needle, as they are mostly on the side away from me, nearest the vet. Thankfully she told me that I was ok, and I managed to put Reba back to standing on the table. A few more gravy bones soon settled her. It was an unexpected reaction, as before she has just stood there calmly, but actually a really good reaction that shows that the nerves are firing well, and messages are getting through.

The healing may even take 12-18 months. It's a long term recovery, and my two main wishes are that her left leg lifts better and not be scuffing her nails, as that will open up more walking areas, and secondly for her to be more coordinated in her movements so that she trots, as that is way more efficient and she will be able to do more than 15 minutes at a time.

Wednesday 5th March

Reba is really trying with her physio exercise, but sometimes she forgets about her rear left leg. I need to get her to go around in circles, but she would just pivot on that leg, so I tried with cones for her to go around. All was good until a point, then her leg was stuck, and she ended up straddling the cone! Bless her, it must be so hard to relearn how to move when before, all her life, it was so natural and you don't even need to think about it.

We went for a lovely sunny walk on the heath. For most of the walk, we barely met a soul, it was so peaceful. We stopped by a bench, and I took the opportunity to get her to walk along it – it's a railway sleeper type. I used my body and held onto the handle of the harness and encouraged her to take a few steps forward on the narrow plank. She did well. The drama happened as we were on the final bit before the car park.

As we ambled along, a collie came to us, no owner in sight – it came from around the corner behind loads of trees/gorse. Well, it was hassling us. After an initial sniff, it was trying to get weight on Reba's body, so I was trying to wave it away, saying 'leave', and then trying to body block it. It was just circling us and being a total pest. I was calling out to find the owner, Reba was circling to get away from it and then she was jumping up at me to get away. Reba has never growled or snapped at another dog, not even a few years ago when she was being mauled by some labradors that did some damage to her. Anyway, I picked her up as she was tired anyway, wobbly and I have to be so careful of her neck movements and dogs pushing her body down. This collie just wouldn't leave us alone, and was jumping up constantly, about 15 times or more, circling us. I'm trying to manoeuvre Reba away from it, and finally saw the owner approach, but then stop at a distance. Despite me asking, then shouting at them to call their dog away, they stood there, watching and laughing, then told me to put my dog down. Grrrr. I did say she was recovering from serious medical issues, and that

I had to pick her up as their dog was harassing us for some time before they came into view. Seriously, this woman still did nothing. I was even trying to use my leg to get this dog away, just short of kicking it – it did cross my mind but then it could have bitten me. Eventually she did get her dog, saying I was overreacting, it was 'just a puppy'. Well, this dog was fully grown, and it doesn't matter what age the dog is, leaving it to harass and jump all over other people is unacceptable, period.

She eventually walked away, cursing and swearing at me, despite it being her dog out of control and thinking it was entertaining just leaving me in the mess that it caused.

That evening, Reba was just lying on the sofa next to me, when she did an unexpected poo! Just one nugget, but still yuck! We've not had any accidents like that for a long time, but it does remind me she is not 100% in control of her bowels yet.

Then when I went to the kitchen, and normally she would stay on the sofa till I came back, I turned around and there she was, at my feet. The monkey had jumped down off the sofa! I hadn't heard her, so not sure if she fell or not, but there is a large dog bed cushion right by the sofa as I have always been worried about her falling off it.

Thursday 6th March

It was hydrotherapy this morning, and new roadworks made the area gridlocked. Very stressful but managed to get there with minutes to spare! Reba was so reluctant to leave my side! She was like a cartoon character, planting her feet wide and refusing to move, the poor hydro lady had to pick her up to take her in. I could hear a load of howls, and the physio lady was passing and said she was looking really happy but being very noisy today!

They have lowered the water level a bit again and even did a small incline so that there was more load on the rear. When you look at the video, you would never guess that there had been any issue with the front legs, they placed perfect every time (although Reba will go on her wrist when she lowers her head to sniff things on her walk, so that may be more to do with the fact that bending down is uncomfortable on her neck). She needed more assistance with her rear but was doing better than last time. She doesn't like it when they are guiding both legs, it makes her wobble more! However, it was improving, and she was stronger than last visit too.

When I chatted after, they said that I will always need to be careful about other dogs as any wrong sudden movement or 'rough and tumble' play could literally dislodge her metalwork/cement and kill her. She cannot ever have any pressure on her neck again.

As for getting her to trot, this may come in time, but until then, Reba struggles for walking more than 15 minutes, as the bunny hopping run and the mental thoughts of where her legs are is very tiring for her. I'm hopeful that this will improve, and if she can learn to co-ordinate her rear legs better, then this may help her stamina too.

Her little friend is over this afternoon for a sleepover. He is gentle so they are good match, and I don't have to worry about them playing. He is literally just sleeping in the sunshine on my patio!

Friday 7th March
Reba really enjoyed her McTimoney today. She didn't need as many adjustments as before – yippee, and she was really good as well, as the first side she offered was her left, even lying on her right-hand side pretty well too, quite unlike before. In fact, it was horrible having to wake her to turn her over!

She is also looking straighter, and her left hip is not as low as before too, so all this effort is working.

Later on, whilst trying to get her better with the nail clippers, I saw that on her front left, the middle two nails are really worn down, shockingly so. It's not quite at the quick (the blood and nerve endings) but I need immediate action to prevent it getting worse.

I've bought some more faux grass to cover the rest of the patio, and I've ordered a bootee without knowing if she will even accept wearing it, so I've got lots of treats ready for when it arrives, and will slowly get her wearing it. Well, that is the plan.

Saturday 8th March

Bumped into a friend and her two dogs as I arrived in the car park. Her older one has a terrible new diagnosis, so we pottered slowly to the cricket ground as this one can't really walk, my one is wobbly, but her other one is fine, thankfully. She had a ball to get her young one to chase, but she ignored it, however Reba obliged with much gusto... she rolled on the way there, and then once she picked it up, she rolled again, but magically kept hold of the ball! She even ran back with it - now this is a dog that rarely retrieves, even with all the training I've tried with her!

The dogs had a lovely mooch, and she is interested in buying the buggy that I borrowed, so that she can at least take the young one out further on walks.

Sunday 9th March

Yesterday I had ordered a set of bootees for Reba, and they arrived. They look quite sturdy, with a rubber base for traction, and Velcro reflective strips around the opening. I was so surprised that she took to them so well. I put one on her front paw and gave a few treats, thinking that after the disaster of the carpel support at the physio, she won't even move. How wrong I was! She happily walked around so I kept it on her for a while, and she lay down to sleep with it on. Success!

I'm wondering if it's the sand from the heath that is causing the friction. Although it's a soft surface, the grains must be grinding against the nail. At least we have a solution now. I took her for a walk later, on the heath and she wasn't bothered by it at all.

Tuesday 11th March

Decided to drive over to the animal feed store, where I used to hold my classes. There is a big, open field, which the majority is fenced off for sheep, but there is still a good part to walk over. The grass is quite tufty, so this really made Reba pick her toes up. She was on the long line (so she kept away from the sheep and electric fence) and had great fun running around. On the last section back towards the car park, I was videoing some short bursts, and when I played it back, it showed her for about two whole strides, slow down from her bunny hopping run, and looked like she did a trot, so alternated her rear legs! This is phenomenal. It may only be a split second, but it's a huge light as it shows that there is something there that she remembers, about how to move as a dog.

I put her boot back on and did a little walk around the shop, where she hoovered up some dropped treats near the pick and mix display. None from the shelf, only those that were on the floor.

Super impressed with her today. The new faux grass arrived too, so that more of the patio is now covered with very thin but softer surface.

Wednesday 12th March

Reba loves the pole work for the physio, probably as she knows she is getting treats which makes her super keen, which in turn is a problem as she tries to race over them. She is turned around and back over the first one literally as she is chewing the food, ready to get to the other side for another treat. It's quite an effort to slow her down but she is doing better and not knocking them over quite as much.

Thursday 13th March

We met her friend, Byron, with his mum today for a walk, and headed over to Puttenham as that means we can do a shorter walk, not too hilly, and they have a coffee truck there so we can still have time to chat whilst the dogs mooch around. Reba still tires quickly, but it doesn't stop her having zoomies and rolling in muck. She had a great time, but she still got to have a lovely sniff around as we had a coffee. Mind you, once they both realised we had a little cake each, they stuck to us like glue, staring up at us, willing us to drop some.

Not today, lovely, it's not good for you – not good for me but at least it's not toxic for me!

She had her McTimoney this afternoon and again settled well into the massage. It must feel so good getting the tension out of her right side. She does little sighs of contentment during the treatment, a sign of approval.

Saturday 15th March

Visited Nana Cake today, and my nephews were there too. They had not seen Reba since before the accident and from the sounds of it, had not really been told about her. Reba was a bit unstable on the kitchen floor, but we stayed mostly in the living room (apart from when we ate lunch), so the carpet was fine for her. There is a bigger than normal drop down from the kitchen level to the outside garden, about 10-12 inches, so I was lifting her up and down each time she went in and out of the garden. However, one time when I opened the back door, she flew out herself, even with the big drop, and landed almost like a cat, but managed to stay upright on all four paws. Very impressed, but my heart was in my mouth. With her front paw still knuckling at times, it is a worry that she will fall, as just the other side of the back door is the wall to the garage.

Sunday 16th March

Got up before Reba, so her normal thing is to roll over on her back to get a chest rub, but today she hadn't realised just how against the edge of her bed she was and managed to roll right over and out of her bed, landing on her belly! She looked so shocked!

I took her up to the Mount for a walk. We don't go there often as there is very limited parking, and it can be incredibly muddy and slippery, but recently the weather has been dry. The first section is road, as you cannot park by the entrance, and it is a series of fields on a slope with the most incredible views – you can see the London skyline, Heathrow airport and beyond. We just walked around the first field and she loved it, so we will go back there before it gets muddy again.

Monday 17th March

We have a few quiet days this week. No plans, so will just crack on with her physio, some short walks and then see how she does ahead of her next hydrotherapy session later this week.

Thursday 20th March

She did so well in the water treadmill today. They upped the block times by 90 seconds, and she needed less intervention than last time, as her back legs were not crossing over as much. Once she gets going, she gets a good rhythm going, but she does like to be a bit lazy and default to easy, instead of correct! Despite this, they are really pleased, saying that every two weeks is working well and no need to increase this, and she is still making improvements.

Friday 21st March

We bumped into the family with the three spaniels that we know. We last saw them a few weeks ago, but today they commented on how much more stable Reba is, that she is looking stronger in her hind end, and she has a better look in her eyes – more full of life. This was so heartwarming to hear, as being with her every day, it can be hard to see these things, so having others spot these differences is amazing, and motivating.

Saturday 22nd March

I had a medical appointment today, so had to leave her alone for longer than we had practiced. There was nothing I could do about this, but had the camera on her for when I could have a look. She was lying right by the door, but relaxed with her head facing away, so not all bad. She obviously was not loving it, but she was not showing anxiety – well, the times I could check the camera. This is a huge improvement from before, it's the first time she's had a substantial time alone from me since the accident too.

Thursday 27th March

We had her follow-up physio appointment today, and the first thing was to see her move in a walk outside. The physio was very impressed and was happy to see so much progress. Reba had her boot on, as there was paving out there, but she still could see enough to be able to assess her. Inside, she then checked her knuckling responses, and these have improved too. She was very complimentary about how much better Reba is, and the work I have put in. See, professionals know when you have been doing your homework or not... I could always tell which of my clients had not bothered, the dogs tell us by their actions.

Anyway, Reba, now bootless, was climbing over the poles in the room, and could show that she can do it, but it's hard for her. The more we can go slowly, the better and stronger her responses will be. It is there, just not consistent, but this will help overall. We have some exercises to hopefully help with the front paw, as the dragging of this is close to causing injuries to her skin and nails, and so if we can get the nerves working better, then this will hopefully improve to a much better level.

The physio wanted to get some video of her walking slowly outside again, without the boot, to show the head surgeon of her progress, and we are back to see her in six weeks.

I'm so happy that it's positive. She can see a marked difference, and deep down, Reba can do it, so that is really positive. We just need to get her brain sending the messages more strongly and more often, so it becomes instinctual again. She said the lack of trotting may take a year or so to improve, as we need to get her hind legs moving independently more, and by that time, we will definitely know what state Reba will be in permanently, but we are a long way off that for now, and so there is every chance of more improvements to her gait and movement.

Friday 28th March

McTimoney was really happy with her today. Reba started the session by playing tug with a toy, something she rarely does so we let it carry on for about a minute, which is longer that she has ever done! Talk about timing...

Anyway, she needed less adjustments on her hips, as they were not as bad as before, and with the massage, they noticed that where her right side was always overcompensating for the weaker left side, it's normally really tight but today it was less restricting, so less tight. This means that her left side is taking more of the action and weight. It's these differences that make it so important to see the whole dog, and why we've been doing a range of therapies. They all have an important purpose, but each one cannot do all of the things.

Sunday 30th March

Lovely sunny day, so I decided to drive further afield and visit the boardwalk on the nature reserve today. Last time we visited, we were both wrapped up in many layers, and Reba was just in the buggy. Dogs are on lead on the actual boardwalk, and due to the small gaps between the planks. Reba walked slowly for most of it, until she was getting tired and then she was defaulting to the bunny hopping run. I was so proud of her effort, as the path looped quite a way around the ponds. She was concentrating on placing her feet carefully and was using each leg individually. For the last bit, I took her boot off so she could feel the sensation on her paws. The sound of her dragging and scuffing was loud, and it's a real fine balance between what she needs and what I need to protect her. As a reward, I had decided to let her go to the accessible ponds (for the dogs). They are shallow at the edges but do get deeper, well... Reba's standard – not so much for tall dogs! Since the accident, I've been so worried about her falling over in the water, going under and not able to get up quickly and drowning, however she is so much better now and more stable. The first few times, fab, I caught some video of her splashing around and falling over on the dry edge. What wasn't on video was just after when she fell over in the shallows, her head went under momentarily, but she got up pretty quickly. That was enough for my nerves, so we walked along the path back to the car.

I can't tell you just how much of a milestone this has been for us. I never thought that we would get to this point where she can splash in the shallows, off lead.

Her physio will be very happy today too as there was much more slower walking, which is our next challenge, slowing everything down.

Thursday 3rd April

Bit of a booking drama so we have double therapies today, not ideal but we will see how she goes.

First off, it's McTimoney treatment at home. Reba's hips are much more level this time, and only a few spinal adjustments needed too. She settled into her massage, only getting up just before the end as she decided she'd had enough. Normally she feels that she needs a whole day of massage, so she must be feeling better.

We had an hour's rest before getting into the car and battling all the new roadworks to get to the hydrotherapy centre. Here, again, she did well. I warned them that she had a treatment already today, so either she would be super supple, or tired. They kept the timing the same, so 11 minutes split into four chunks, but they lowered the water (less support) and put on a small incline (loading the weight on the rear legs) so she had to work harder this time, with less help. She apparently was a bit perturbed about this, but managed well, and got over her laziness. She likes it when the water and the therapists are helping her, as it's easier for her. She needs to be kept pushing, as that is the only way she is going to improve.

I'm so proud of how she has coped today, and the delight didn't end there.

At night, I get her to go out for a toilet before bed, and after lying on the sofa for the evening, normally her legs are all over the place, she is crossing her hind legs, tripping herself up, her rear legs going off at all angles apart from the direction they should, and she ends up wobbling all over the garden as her body takes her to a different place to where she was heading. Tonight was different, as she looked much more stable when she scuppered onto the lawn. Her rear legs stayed more in line, and her body even stayed in the one direction – so excited to see this. It may not seem much but for us, this is HUGE!

You would think that she would be tired, but she got up a few times in the night, but it was a quick 'bed' cue to get her back to settle again.

Friday 4th April

Reba is making a more determined effort every day. It's not always working, such as today when I was encouraging her onto the sofa next to me. Often, she makes it, a few times she even has a steady landing on all her legs, but like today, her back end just didn't reach the cushions, so she was just on by her front paws. You can see her making judgements before she leaps, and this is all working her brain and sending the messages from there to her body, to control how it moves. We will continue with this, and then maybe even progress to jumping down - we still have the dog bed by the sofa for a step/soft landing. She's not ready for the height of my bed, so I'm lifting her up onto it whilst I read for a bit in bed, then have to carry her down to hers. I somehow think that secretly she enjoys this and probably pretends to never be able to do this on her own, but only time will tell if she is strong enough, and her front paw can take any strain. She is keen to jump out of the car, though, when we arrive to her walking spots! I don't let her though.

I won't let her try the staircase yet either, so again, more lifting and carrying every day, but this can only be tackled if and when she is ever ready, which may be never.

All I can do is to shower her with love and be impressed on how far she has come. We have at least another seven months of this journey, the weekly routine of physio, hydro, massages and more, despite the soaring costs, as she deserves every opportunity to thrive. After a year, that could well be the most she will heal, so we will just have to deal with any clumsiness or disability then. Of course, I want her paws to stop dragging and scuffing, so that she doesn't have to wear the boot, and not be restricted on surfaces we go on, which will open up more walks. And if she can learn to trot, and run better, more like a normal dog, then she will have more stamina to be out for longer too. Right now, she is still tiring after 15 minutes, and I'm not getting the exercise either!

I often think back to that horrendous evening, finding her nearly dead in the darkness of my garden, and even though she has a long way to go, I can see just how far she has come. She's independent, enjoying getting out and about, and be able to do things for herself again.

Head traumas and spinal injuries affect every patient differently, whatever species, and I've no doubt that she has some permanent damage. What I am super thankful for is that she is still the softest, caring, sweetest personality and the trauma did not change her in that way.

She's been my companion, best friend, and business partner. She's changed my career, and been so loved and I am truly thankful and blessed I get to spend more time with her.

She's made me a better person, one that is more tolerant (she hates it if I raise my voice!), and I wouldn't change a thing... well, maybe the events of THAT night, but then I wouldn't be here and adding more skills to my career, based on her life.

Thank you, my sassy Reba, keep on fighting forward.

ABOUT THE AUTHOR

Jo Sellers is an award winning ABTC Accredited Trainer and a Certified Separation Anxiety Behaviourist.

Pippin Pets Dog Training was established in 2015 at the same time her dog Reba joined the family. This cheeky Cocker Spaniel/Bichon Frise crossbreed led her to specialise in Separation Anxiety after helping Reba overcome her fear of being home alone.

Helping dogs overcome Separation Anxiety is now the principal part of her business and online support for other trapped at home owners, and she has helped hundreds of other dogs and owners.

In 2024, Reba's freak accident shook her world, and a long road of recovery loomed ahead. She took on the challenge, learning about dog's biology and motion, the various rehabilitation therapies, and alongside the many specialists, helped her dog to learn to walk again

Jo regularly studies and learns from other amazing professionals to keep up to date and learn new skills and techniques in order to provide her clients with the best support and guidance.

For more information about our books and services, please visit

www.greencatbooks.com

Green Cat Books

www.ingramcontent.com/pod-product-compliance
Lightning Source LLC
Chambersburg PA
CBHW070445090426
42735CB00012B/2463